Forms of the Novel in the Work of Camilo José Cela

Forms of the Novel in the Work of Camilo José Cela

David W. Foster

University of Missouri Studies Volume XLIII

University of Missouri Press
Columbia · Missouri

Library of Congress Catalog
Card Number 67–63071

Printed and bound in the United States of America

Estas que me dictó ideas sonoras
culta sí, aunque bien amada, Nana
– ¡oh docto colega! – en las pur-
púreas horas que es rosas la alba y
la verdad no vana, escucha . . .

CONTENTS

Introduction

UNTIL very recently, the Spanish novel of the twentieth century has been relatively isolated from trends and innovations in the novel outside of Spain. One of the leading critics of the Spanish novel, José María Castellet, contrasts the generation of novelists since 1956 with those of the generation who began to write immediately after the Civil War:

> Dos generaciones de novelistas han surgido en España después de la guerra civil (1936–1939). La primera de ellas, formada en su mayor parte por hombres que hicieron la guerra al lado de los vencedores, apareció a lo largo de la década de los años cuarenta y su mayor mérito consistió en reavivar una tradición novelística que había sido poco prolífica y de desigual calidad en los años que precedieron a la guerra civil. La obra de estos escritores se caracteriza por una apreciable calidad literaria, con escasa preocupación por los problemas técnicos del arte narrativo, y por una intención realista de tipo general que, sin embargo, no se propone la expresión de una estética realista determinada, contentándose, en líneas generales, con una adscripción a los movimientos literarios que giran en torno a los métodos narrativos del realismo crítico.[1]

As traditional as the novel may have seemed from a technical point of view during the first decade and a half following the Civil War, it is still noteworthy that it was able to flourish, given its immediate antecedents in the twentieth century.

The Spanish novelists of this century began, as did novelists in other parts of Europe, by attempting to free the novel from the strong tradition of realism that had developed in the nineteenth century. The realist novel in Spain is singular in that it makes no significant contribution to the development of novelistic technique. While it is true that Benito Pérez Galdós is a great novelist, it is difficult to speak of his novels as anything other than a brilliant fusion of the various techniques and tendencies that had sprung from the English, French, and Russian novels of his period. However, when Galdós is compared with Spanish novelists contemporaneous to him, one can see that this was no mean accomplishment for one who was so scorned by his country's intellectual elite.

The Spanish novel of the last century is also singular in its refusal to go much beyond the boundaries of realism. Naturalism, either as an esthetic or an ideological program for the novel, was rejected in the main by the writers in the Spanish tradition. One looks in vain in the works of the so-called Spanish Naturalists, Emilia Pardo Bazán and Vicente Blasco Ibáñez, for the sophistication and secure orientation of the English, French, and American writers.[2]

Therefore, the flowering of realism is all the more prominent in Spain because of this lack of contributions to the tradition and of extensive development beyond generally limited confines. Realism as an orientation has succeeded in providing a thread that runs throughout the twentieth-century Spanish novel. It is an orientation that has not been fully superseded, in spite of a violent reaction to realism in the opening years of this century in the form of the novels of the Generation of '98. Miguel de Unamuno, Azorín, Pío Baroja, and Ramón del Valle-Inclán represent in their novels a collective reaction to the mimetic esthetic of the novel.

The reaction against realism in Europe as a whole concentrated its attack on the problem of characterization. The realist novelists tried to create a situation that represented a microcosmic enactment of life, placing characters in that situation to better observe and detail their multiple and complex reactions to the web of human circumstance. The younger novelists, on the other hand, took exception to the necessity for seeing man as he functions in terms of social interaction and to the belief that such is, indeed, the most reliable means of revealing the nature of man.[3]

The reaction against the procedure of the realists has taken many forms. Indeed, because of the diverse nature of any literature contemporary to the critic, it appears that there are more trends or tendencies contrary to realism than he can attempt to enumerate. This is a self-evident truism, since it would be absurd to speak of a tradition that continues realism and that breaks with it. If there is a continuation of the realist novel, it has been inextricably intertwined with techniques and forms that were developed originally to renounce realism. In terms of the major problem of characterization, one may note the following major developments.[4]

One not-so-surprising development has been the novel that is ironical in its approach to the autonomous world posited by the realists. Virginia Woolf's audacious *Orlando* comes immediately to mind as a novel that completely shatters the autonomy of the character's personality, thereby indulging in an irony against the reader who expects Orlando to be a man neatly defined by a single set of traits and characteristics and firmly anchored in a specific time and place wherein he would act out the detailed part accorded him by the benevolent author. Such is not the case, and the heavy hand of the author rearranges what quickly ceases to be a slice of life in order to present more forcibly her vision of man. In the Spanish novel, Valle-Inclán's and Unamuno's works employ much the same procedure. The end result is a novel that is less the harmonious union of the omniscient author's commentary and the characters' diligent enactment of the human comedy than the often too obvious demonstration of reality by an author who is not content to reveal mankind merely in terms of verisimilar externals.

Stream of consciousness is a technique that has come to be one of the most prominent characteristics of the contemporary novel. In part, it satisfies the author's concern to eliminate the point of view that depicts him as a marginal observer who somehow has a perception of events beyond that of any of the characters. In the novels that use stream of consciousness, the author, in abandoning any pretense of being merely an overly perceptive observer, readily succeeds in making his point of view superfluous by substituting for it a perspective that is projected externally from within the mind of one or more characters. The internal monologue of a man's mind replaces the author-character dichotomy, which is frustrating as an attempt to portray convincingly the interior man. Stream of consciousness has become a technique so all-pervading in the contemporary novel that it would be difficult to describe all of its ramifications and manifestations. Humphrey's basic definition serves as the most reliable orientation available:

> The stream-of-consciousness novel is identified most quickly by its subject matter. This, rather than its techniques, its purposes, or its themes, distinguishes it. Hence, the novels that are said to use the stream-of-consciousness *technique* to a considerable degree prove, upon analysis, to be novels which have as their essential subject matter the consciousness of one or more characters; that is, the depicted consciousness serves as a screen on which the material in these novels is presented.[5]

It is apparent by what I have said up to this point that the major developments in the contemporary novel have been attempts to free character and the devices or techniques employed to depict and analyze character from the narrow confines of the naturalistic situations favored by the previous novelistic traditions. Contemporary novelists have, generally speaking, set for themselves the task of exploring the recesses of the human mind in order to relate man as a complex emotional and sensitive individual to more than simply the physical and sociological aspects of his circumstance. The two tendencies that I have just described, the novel as an expressionistic conceit and as stream of consciousness, are similar in their probing of the individual beyond the surface. However, both essentially maintain the integrity of the personality as something the reader is able to grasp on the basis of its presentation at any given moment.

Another major development in the contemporary novel has centered around the problem of personality as something that does not exist in the present, but is a set of emotional experiences that transcend the boundaries of chronologic time.[6] Experiments in the realm of time and reality dwell upon the individual as someone who is dominated by a memory that cannot be described in terms of the present, no matter how deeply the unconscious is explored. Rather, man lives through the past, which he cannot escape, and his contact with reality is a contact that is continually evoking for him the past. Man lives his life and reacts in the present as a result of a contingent past. Therefore, the novels in the tradition that has derived from the ideas of Proust and Bergson employ the stream-of-consciousness technique, but in a manner that probes the personality horizontally across the boundaries of mathematical or chronological time as well as in depth. The result is a character who is defined not only by what he thinks *now*, but also by what he saw and felt *then*.

Time plays another role in contemporary literature, extending beyond the exploration of man as a being who is subject to memory as well as to circumstance. Many novelists — Camilo José Cela in Spain is prominent among them — have gone a step further and have denied that man is a product of memory. Instead, time for man as a witness of the development and progression of his personality is a fiction. Time is an artificial concept that possesses reality only in the mechanical movement of the clock. Man exists merely at points in space. He is defined by his physical existence, but his development over a period of measurable time is an unobservable phenomenon. Consequently, Cela and many of the new novelists portray man as a static entity who *is* rather than *is becoming*. Such a viewpoint, however, does not eschew the probing of man in depth; its only common denial is of the existential nature of man. The novels that employ a fragmentation of chronology toward proving the unimportance of chronology, far from representing a return to the realist novel, which in any case did adhere strictly to the popular notion of the unity of time, bespeak in many ways the beginning in the contemporary novel of the exhaustion of the "depth of the personality" cult that has dominated novelists during most of this century.

Before exploring in detail this reaction against internalization of perspective, it is worth noting two additional major developments in the novel that attempt to explore in greater detail the human condition. One is the literature of mythic and symbolic archetypes. While it is true that most universal literature may be interpreted in terms of dominant human archetypes, a group of novels has emerged that represents a definite attempt on the part of the artist—no doubt inspired by Jung's theories of the collective unconscious— to elaborate a prominent myth in the structure of his novel.[7] D. H. Lawrence's *Plumed Serpent* and James Joyce's *Ulysses* are good examples of this practice, and contemporary Latin-American literature affords any number of examples.

Engaged in this approach, the novelist portrays man, not as an isolated entity, but as a participant in the universal history of mankind. Man may be a suffering individual racked with intermittent anguish and despair, joy and hope. Nevertheless, as an individual he embodies and repeats the collective experience of the human race. Therefore, it is not surprising that the novel of the collective unconscious has merged in many instances with the novel of social realism. Ignazio Silone's *Pane e vino*, for example, employs the Christ-figure within the framework of the universal class struggle unique to the vision of the Marxist novelists. In the case of both the general tradition of the collective unconscious and the limited instance of the works of the social realists, the portrayal of personality strives to achieve breadth and depth by the use of general characteristics of the contemporary novel as a whole. However, since the novel of the mythic archetype places its interest and emphasis on meanings external to the individual, personality portrayal is deliberately curtailed at many points in the narratives.

Existentialism represents the one other great contemporary preoccupation with man as an individual.[8] Unlike the novels of the collective unconscious, the existential novel attempts to portray a character who strives to free himself from circumstantial entanglements in order to glorify his sense of uniqueness. The novels of Jean-Paul Sartre, *La nausée* for example, are perhaps the most widely known, having served as bellwethers for a generation of writers of similar philosophic and technical persuasions. As a thematic orientation, existentialism has had immeasurable impact on contemporary literature, and many critics' understanding of literature is in danger of seeing the whole of the Western tradition in terms of the existential ethic. With regard to twentieth-century works, there is little doubt that a particular form of the novel has emerged from the meeting between artist and existential thinker. These works are characterized by the restricted point of view of a few prominent characters, by the eschewing of temporal and physical setting, and by the limitations imposed upon social interaction as an element of plot. The character is surrounded by an external world that is little more than an infrequently perceived haze, and his internal monologue while in the processes of perception, choice, and becoming is foregrounded in passages that read like the deliberation of the ages.[9]

Existentialism has touched Spanish literature in the novels of Alejandro Núñez Alonso. However, it is not surprising that contemporary Spanish letters do not betray existentialist trends to the extent that other national literatures do. The conservative influence of Roman Catholicism on Spanish thought is such that the critic searches in vain for a movement equivalent even to Catholic existentialism, and it is worth noting that Núñez Alonso resides in Mexico. Nevertheless, for the critic whose approach is topical and dependent upon the unconscious psychological attitudes of the writer, existential trends have been found in the novels of Cela, Ana María Matute, Juan Goytisolo, Miguel Delibes, and Antonio Buero Vallejo, to name a few of the more prominent writers.

José María Castellet, in the article previously quoted, goes on to speak of a younger generation of writers in Spain that has emerged since 1956. One notes

> el éxito que entre los jóvenes novelistas españoles ha tenido la narración objetiva (de procedencia americana y que nada tiene que ver con la "literatura del objeto" o "école du regard" francesa). Conocida por ellos a través de la divulgación hecha por algunos ensayistas y críticos franceses (Sartre y C.-E. Magny, p.e.), la narración objetiva, que describe la acción de la novela como lo haría una cámara cinematográfica, sin intervenciones ni comentarios del autor, les ha permitido evadir, en parte, la dura presión de la censura. [. . . Su] descripción del mundo, de la sociedad española actual, está hecha en función de la no aceptación, del rechazo absoluto de una realidad social determinada, por una parte, y de su esperanza de cambio, de transformación de esa realidad social, por otra.[10]

Castellet's analysis of the preoccupations of the younger Spanish novelists incorporates three basic tendencies of the contemporary novel that may be discussed together as a reaction against or a development parallel to the major concern of the contemporary novel for man as an individual and his inner personality.

The first of these basic tendencies is what Castellet refers to as the influence of American behaviorism. Behaviorism is the American contribution to the theory of psychology (see the professional publications of B. F. Skinner and his novel *Walden Two*), a theory that has influenced the American school of linguistics and the American novel. John Dos Passos' *Manhattan Transfer* and *U.S.A.* have often been referred to as prototypes of the behaviorist novel that have influenced European writers. Mention should also be made of Aldous Huxley's *Point Counterpoint* as a European example of the tendency in the novel to study man as a set of actions and reactions, responses to given situations and dilemmas. In many ways superficially reminiscent of the realist novel, the behaviorist novel observes rather than probes, documents rather than analyzes. Character is seen in terms of individuals, but of individuals who can be examined as the reflection of situation. Behaviorism advances the theory that the patterns of man's behavior are exclusively the result of the decisions he has had to make in the face of certain formative circumstances. Man's inner being, to the extent that it may exist, is the conscious attempt to understand and to rationalize the pattern of the individual's unconscious reflexes, emotional and actional. Man, therefore, does not possess free will and usually cannot consciously alter his behavioral personality. The behaviorist novels chart his personality as the result of the experiences to which he has been subjected and the decisions he has been forced to make. As a result, man is seen externally and, often, fragmentarily. He may be seen against the texture of society in an attempt to criticize the society he exemplifies, or he may be seen merely as an animal adrift in a society of equally behavioristically determined unfortunates. As I shall point out in this study, several of Cela's works follow a procedure similar to the approach of the behaviorist novel. Another Spaniard, Rafael Sánchez Ferlosio (*El Jarama*), might also be mentioned here.

During the years following World War II, the Italian cinema and later the Italian novel began to demonstrate an orientation subsequently labeled neo-realism.[11] Concerned with the state of Italian society, these artists attempted to depict the nature and origins of middle-class morality and what they saw as its decay. As early as 1920, Alberto Moravia's *Gli indifferenti* had probed this subject, and his later novels, along with those of Vasco Pratolini (*Il quartiere*), examine the relationship between man and his society. In general, these novels, aside from an intermittent commingling with social realism, concentrate on the individual as he attempts to realize himself in a society that threatens to destroy him, not so much because society is the stronger of the two in the conflict, but because society—a larger entity with its own dynamic being—has failed to provide man with any transcendent reason for living. Man comes to see, in his circumstance and in the congress of mankind, the futility of hope and the absurdity of his dreams.

Neo-realism is not the Theater of the Absurd, but both drink from the waters of existentialism and express its denial of the transcendency of anything that is not man himself. The neo-realists, however, question the dignity of man as a universal and question the world he has produced. Occasionally, their purpose is to lead to the betterment of man; usually, however, their works are more descriptive than prophetic or programmatic. Juan Goytisolo in Spain, particularly in his important work *Fiestas*, demonstrates the thematic and technical orientation of these writers. Their intent is less the achievement of a coherent vision of mankind and his society than it is the exploration of aspects of both—tentative portrayals of modern man's disillusionment with the value system that has been forced upon him. Their language and style is direct and forceful, and they are more the masters of the concise sketch harboring a bitter truth than of the elaborately drawn panorama of a society. Their characters tend often to be static types rather than fully developed personalities, and their art is one of arousing the reader's perceptions rather than of presenting him with an analysis. The neo-realists most typify the modern tradition, as far as technique is concerned, in their insistence that the novel should present the reader with material which he must analyze on his own, deprived of the extended commentary and suggestions of the author.

A more recent "objective" trend in contemporary fiction is the new novel as it has emerged in France.[12] The new novel pushes to extremes the insistence that the reader observe and the novelist not explain. An outgrowth of perspectivism and Husserlian phenomenalism (for example, Ortega y Gasset's "deshumanización del arte" and Gabriel Miró's prototypic *Figuras de la pasión del Señor*), the approach of the new novel is a rejection of the coherency of reality. Events, time, places, and people are a jumbled stream of visual perceptions for the mind, and the new novel makes a virtue out of the chaos of reality by demanding that the reader undergo in the work of art all of the uncertainty, doubt, and error that surrounds our perceptions of the events and people of daily routine. Chronology is disregarded, pattern replaces plot, and treatment of dialogue deviates from the traditional verisimilitude of conversation. Any commitment or sociological, political, and ethical involvement is eschewed. Reality is reduced to objects we can only imperfectly perceive. This most recent major innovation, exemplified by the novels of Alain Robbe-Grillet or Michel Butor, has brought the novel back to where it stood in the opening years of the twentieth century: faced squarely with the deceptions of the realist novel and with the necessity for developing a form and a technique of fiction that will represent a more modern and a more viable theory of human personality and human experience.

This brief account of some of the major developments in the twentieth-century novel will serve to frame the trends of contemporary Spanish prose fiction.

Despite the strong impetus given the novel in Spain by the Generation of '98 and its literary successors, by the time of the Civil War both post-modernism and the dehumanized traits of *entreguerre* literature were well on their way toward stifling the novel with an exaggeratedly refined aestheticism, belying the vigorous product of an earlier Unamuno and a younger Baroja. That the novel was able to resume the hardiness it had exhibited earlier in the century is due in part to the sociological impact of the Civil War upon the younger generation of writers.[13] But whatever the cause-and-effect relationship may be, it is a fact of history that the first novel to appear and to serve as a leader of postwar trends in the novel was Camilo José Cela's *La familia de Pascual Duarte*, first published in 1942. One critic has spoken of those threshold years, literally a cultural vacuum extending from the end of the war in 1939 to Cela's novel in 1942, in the following terms:

> Desde 1939 se esperaba que una sobresaliente novela naciera. La novela es la manifestación estética más divulgada y popular, y trae siempre un mensaje singular de paz o de guerra. Una guerra civil es asimismo una conmoción espiritual formidable. Mientras dura, no hay que pensar en nada sino en hacer la guerra, pero una vez terminada es natural que la novela aflore como fruto de esa conciencia nacional y ensimismada. No sabíamos que nos traería esa obra esperada. [. . .]
>
> Pues bien, en 1942 aparece *La familia de Pascual Duarte*, novela escrita por Camilo José Cela.[14]

Pérez Minik goes on to speak of the success of Cela's novel and the multiplicity of titles that followed in its wake. Saying that Cela's novel opened a floodgate may be a bit too theatrical, yet it is the only way to describe the never-ending stream of novels, good, bad, and indifferent, from which the Spanish reading public of today may choose. It is no surprise to find that the literary prizes are often the reader's only guide.[15]

Nevertheless, no one would want to deny that out of these numbers have come authors and titles that promise to make Spain, if not a leader in the European novel, at least part of European trends. William J. Grupp has observed within the larger context of the intellectual currents of postwar Spain,

> Narrative prose is the most important, most dynamic, most promising genre in Spain today. There has been a great deal of discussion of a "renacimiento" of the Spanish novel, and the point is rapidly being reached at which this can be considered to be literally true, to be something more than an expression of wishful thinking. On the basis of number alone, the novel and the short story are certainly representative of the genre which is most active. The quality of the Spanish novel is uneven; many novels are published without any apparent justification on artistic, stylistic or speculative grounds. But the same criticism can be made of the literature of any nation. The fact that there is an increasing number of young authors who show great promise and have an impressive array of achievements behind them, is, however, a much more valid and encouraging criterion than the sheer numbers involved. . . .
>
> The group born between 1920 and 1930, during the

Republic and the Civil War, holds great promise for the future of the Spanish novel. Among them are Juan Goytisolo, Castillo Puche, Ignacio Aldecoa, Jesús Fernández Santos, Sánchez Ferlosio, Ana María Matute and Elena Soriano. These are the outstanding members of the younger generation, a thoughtful, serious group of young people with a great deal of talent, conscious, deliberate novelists whose mission is to assure Spanish literature a high place among the world's literatures.[16]

Among these young writers, many of whom already have impressive publication records, Camilo José Cela is the acknowledged leader of the postwar generation and is its most accomplished and best-known representative. Although Cela's reception in 1957 into the Royal Spanish Academy has undoubtedly caused him to lose favor with the ever-present and more rebellious younger vanguard, such an acceptance is a significant recognition of Cela's importance.

Cela's works have been the subject of much controversy, debate, and some serious critical study.[17] While it is too early for any of the issues to have been resolved, their very presence bears witness to the central position of this author in any discussion of what the novel is or should be in Spain today. For not only has Cela been responsible for revitalizing the Spanish novel by giving it impetus with a series of artistically excellent works, but he has chosen as well to make his career one of a complete re-examination and reconsideration of the novel as an art form. Cela's consistent refusal to adhere to any a priori assumptions concerning the novel and his insistence on being the most unpredictable writer since the tempestuous Unamuno have not endeared him to all literary critics.

Before proceeding to an examination of Cela's works, mention of the critical orientation of this study may prove of some assistance to the reader. My primary intent is to discuss the novels in order to underline the "proteic" nature of the structure of Cela's writings. The justification for such single-mindedness is that Cela, in his position as Spain's leading postwar novelist, has created much controversy by the form of his novels. Thus, my approach is descriptive rather than historical. The four other book-length studies of Cela's fiction have contributed greatly to our understanding of his novelistic world and of its themes, language, and devices.[18] Discussion surrounding Cela's novels has made it obvious that the time has come for a study that will lay the groundwork for an examination of Cela's works and the contemporary novel as an art form. One reviewer,[19] while applauding Alonso Zamora Vicente's sympathetic appraisal of Cela's total literary production, has lamented the lack of an extended study of Cela's novel from the point of view of a series of experiments in novelistic technique. Yet, with the possible exception of Olga Prjevalinsky's work, which is confined to a discussion of *La catira*, no critic has undertaken an extensive study of the novelistic forms that Cela has employed to present his vision of mankind. This study attempts to provide such an approach.

The critical vocabulary employed derives mainly from New Criticism and neo-Aristotelianism. Both are primarily American developments in critical theory, and their adherents have refined their tools in the fertile fields of American, British, and, to a lesser extent, French literature.[20] Therefore, many basic ideas are the direct result of developments in the literature produced during the period of formation and maturity of the leading spokesmen of both groups. It is not surprising that relatively little pre-twentieth-century literature has been studied from the point of view of the new critic and that much of the latter's vocabulary and methods reflects the pattern of contemporary imaginative literature. The close relationship between the literature and the criticism as they have developed together, aside from the fact that many of the new critics are both artists and scholars, may be seen in the often disconcerting phenomenon whereby it is difficult to ascertain if the critic's approach has been determined by the work in question or has been imposed upon it. Such is the case, for example, with the archetypal approach.[21] Does the critic see all literature as archetypal, from *Beowulf* to *The*

Alexandria Quartet, or does he discuss archetypes with reference only to that literature written by authors apparently inspired by Jung? Any critical theory, including New Criticism and neo-Aristotelianism, is hampered by the necessary belief that its techniques are the most refined and the most appropriate.

This study of Cela's novels agrees with the idea that the critic should be guided in his approach by what he finds and by what he can demonstrate convincingly with reference to the works themselves. Cela's novels are a critic's delight in that the author has followed so many different procedures that have resulted, in turn, in so many different forms. If nothing else, Cela has become Spain's most restless and versatile novelistic technician. The multiplicity of facets represented in Cela's nine novels has given rise to this study, which is necessarily oriented toward the discussion, in each case, of a particular form. Although the result appears reminiscent of Northrup Frye's a priori categories ("archetypes of the novel"), the orientation I have given each chapter derives from the form of the novel under consideration. Within each chapter, my procedure has been to describe the form of that novel and to examine some related topics, particularly the relationship between content and form. Controversies surrounding the individual novels have served as a point of departure for the examination of the rationale and the apparent justification for the structural design chosen by the author. In each case, the treatment of the work was designed to contribute to an over-all understanding of Cela's concept of the novel.

1

La familia de Pascual Duarte:

THE NOVEL IN A TRADITIONAL FORM

La familia de Pascual Duarte[1] is Camilo José Cela's first novel and his most popular. With its publication, Cela, then in his mid-twenties, began his career as a novelist, probably little realizing the impact this one book was to have upon the languishing novel of postwar Spain. While Cela's later work is considerably more mature, *Pascual Duarte* remains in the foreground as the youthful but energetic and meaningful touchstone for all of his future novels.

Plot

Pascual Duarte is supposedly the publication of a sheaf of handwritten papers left by the executed murderer Pascual Duarte. According to his own statements, Duarte's purposes are to relate his life so that others may profit from his mistakes and to expiate his crime. The autobiography is loosely chronological, Pascual describing the mean circumstances of his birth and childhood and facts about his family, his two wives, and his sister's lover *El Estirao*. The highlights of the narrative, which have been the source of greatest interest to the commentators, are the frank and candid descriptions of the violent killings of *La Yegua*, the mare whose high spirits cause his wife to abort; of *La Chispa*, his pet dog, shot after an altercation with *El Estirao* in which Pascual's manliness is put in doubt; of *El Estirao*, not only the lover of Pascual's sister, but also of Pascual's wife; of Lola, Pascual's wife, strangled for her affair with *El Estirao*; and, finally, of Pascual's mother, in Pascual's tormented mind the source of his misery as a human being for having borne him and for the chaos that her evil ways have brought upon him. However, it is not for these murders that Pascual is condemned to die, but for the political murder of don Jesús González de la Riva, Conde de Torremejía, a member of the local gentry. This latest crime is never described, and Pascual's narrative ends abruptly with the stabbing of his mother. However, don Jesús is casually mentioned several times, and Pascual's narrative is dedicated to his memory. Pascual is in his late fifties when he is executed, probably in late 1936.

Formal and Structural Considerations

FORMAL ELEMENTS

Cela has willfully destroyed the normal pattern of the novel in *Pascual Duarte* whereby an explaining author mediates between the reader and content. It is difficult to establish exactly what factors have been placed between the reader and the events described. However, since the identification and evaluation of those factors are essential to the credibility of the narrative, it is necessary to attempt an identification of the various narrative levels.

The author has couched his narrative in the familiar autobiographical form in which a specific individual presents to the observer-reader a series of events as witnessed and recorded from a unilateral point of view. Such an approach imposes certain limitations on the narrative while at the same time granting the author certain liberties of orientation. By employing this structural orientation he intends, in so far as it is possible, to recede, perhaps even to disappear, from the narrative. The object is, by means of a series of likely or credible attributions, to place the responsibility for the narrative in the hands of another and to avoid the impression that the author is inventing rather than relating.[2] Such a desire may be attributed to an attempt to achieve objectivity and a reader-content rather than a reader-author-content relationship. Cela would have us believe that a real, historic Pascual Duarte is speaking directly to us, rather than a Pascual Duarte who is a figment of Cela's imagination. The attempt on the part of the storyteller to avoid direct responsibility for the tales he spins is as old as storytelling itself. It remains effective because we cannot argue with the storyteller and because his source, imaginative or historic, is inaccessible to us at the moment of telling. On the other hand, the desire on the part of the author to appear to be avoiding a personal interpretation is more recent and corresponds to a desire for objectivity in art that originated in certain aspects of nineteenth-century realism.[3] Cela is not unique in his use of self-distancing in *Pascual Duarte*. The novel, within its particular structural etiquette, is quite traditional.

Dispensing with the fiction proposed by the novel that there is no author, we may begin by identifying two external layers: the reader and the author, the obvious *sine qua non* of any novel. The first internal layer is that represented by the *Transcriptor* who both opens and closes the novel. The effect is to enclose the narrative within a set of boundaries represented by an individual whose only attachment to the material is his interest in its content and its dissemination. He serves to authenticate and to substantiate the source of the central narrative, although he can testify neither to its accuracy nor to its sincerity. Such a procedure also allows Cela to solve the problem of how to justify the beginning and the conclusion. The *Transcriptor* begins his transcription at the point the manuscript begins and concludes it at the point the manuscript ends. That the transcription ends precisely when the narrative reaches its dramatic peak is indeed a lamentable fact, but the *Transcriptor* is not to be blamed. He has, if we are to believe him, done his unsuccessful best to find the remaining fragments. Thus, Cela may conclude his narrative at a climactic and meaningful point without having to worry about the reader's interest in the ensuing loose-ends operation represented by the time-worn device of the Epilogue.

The use of the *Transcriptor* fulfills another function that corresponds solely to the particular demands of content imposed by *Pascual Duarte.* If the novel pretends to be a reflection of reality, it is highly unlikely that a man of Pascual Duarte's acknowledged birth and education would produce the work as we see it. The *Transcriptor* brings to Duarte's humble attempts some semblance of grammatical Spanish and serves to maintain the veracity of the writer's low birth and lack of education. Cela adds to the authenticity and palpable reality of the intermediary with the *Transcriptor*'s detailed description of his fruitless search for more manuscript in a pharmacist's shop, related in the *Otra Nota del Transcriptor* that follows the abrupt breaking-off of Pascual's narrative.

One would assume that the immediate antecedent to the *Transcriptor* is Pascual Duarte. This is not the case, however, since it would put the two in communication and throw a certain unwanted responsibility upon the former. The manuscript must necessarily have been lost and found. Originally, Pascual addressed his effort to one señor don Joaquín Barrera López Mérida, into whose hands the manuscript passed and who bequeathed it at his death to a convent. How the papers got to the pharmacy where they were subsequently found by the *Transcriptor* remains a mystery. Nevertheless, the only mediating presence is that of Barrera. Cryptically alluded to as a friend of don Jesús, Pascual's final victim, Barrera remains otherwise unidentified in the narrative. Addressing the manuscript to Barrera serves to lend a certain mystery and implies an appeal to a higher order. The dedication to Barrera suggests that the narrative be considered an act of confession in which Duarte attempts to explain to Barrera, perhaps at one time his benefactor, why he is as he is. It is not a public confession, but an attempt at exculpation before the only authority Pascual seems to recognize. Don Jesús, in fact, is the only other person not of Duarte's class mentioned in the autobiography. Since don Jesús is dead, Duarte turns to the only friend of don Jesús whom he can recall.

The semblance of privacy is enhanced by Duarte's dedication of his autobiography "A la memoria del insigne patricio don Jesús González de la Riva, Conde de Torremejía, quien al irlo a rematar el autor de este escrito, le llamó Pascualillo y sonreía." (p. 23). Therefore, it is possible to conclude that Duarte's opening sentence, "Yo, señor, no soy malo, aunque no me faltarían motivos para serlo" (p. 25), is directed exclusively to Barrera. Not only has the author (Cela) retreated from the scene, but he has as well made the reader a shameful intruder.

Little need be said of Pascual Duarte himself as narrator at this point. He serves to introduce the principal characters who, in belonging to "la familia de Pascual Duarte," may be considered significant and important. Since it is Pascual who serves as the central point of intelligence, we may draw only partial and one-sided conclusions as to the true nature of these characters, on the basis of the often haphazard and certainly prejudiced information Pascual Duarte offers.

After Pascual's narrative is concluded and in order to authenticate the transmittal of the original manuscript into Barrera's hands, the *Transcriptor* provides us with testimony from two witnesses, the prison priest and a guard. The testimony of the two witnesses disagrees over the reason for Pascual's comportment in the face of death and underlines the difficulty in knowing what to believe concerning the events and emotions described. According to the priest,

> Dispuso los negocios del alma con un aplomo y una serenidad que a mí me dejaron absorto y pronunció delante de todos, cuando llegó el momento de ser conducido al patio, un *¡Hágase la voluntad del Señor!* que mismo nos dejara maravillados con su edificante humildad. ¡Lástima que el enemigo le robase sus últimos instantes, porque si no, a buen seguro que su muerte habría de haber sido tenida como santa! Ejemplo de todos los que la pre-

> senciamos hubo de ser (hasta que perdiera el dominio, como digo), y provechosas consecuencias para mi dulce ministerio de la cura de almas, hube de sacar de todo lo que vi. ¡Qué Dios lo haya acogido en su santo seno! (p. 181)

The guard writes,

> En cuanto a su muerte, sólo he de decirle que fue completamente corriente y desgraciada y que aunque al principio se sintiera flamenco y soltase delante de todo el mundo un *¡Hágase la voluntad del Señor!* que nos dejó como anonadados, pronto se olvidó de mantener la compostura. A la vista del patíbulo se desmayó y cuando volvió en sí, tales voces daba de que no quería morir y de que lo que hacían con él no había derecho, que hubo de ser llevado a rastras hasta el banquillo. Allí besó por última vez un crucifijo que le mostró el Padre Santiago, que era el capellán de la cárcel y mismamente un santo, y terminó sus días escupiendo y pataleando, sin cuidado ninguno de los circunstantes, y de la manera más ruin y más baja que un hombre puede terminar; demostrando a todos su miedo a la muerte. (p. 185)

Both accounts are colored by the nature of the informants' personalities; the priest emphasizes the confession, and the guard emphasizes the natural but "unmanly" fear of death Pascual demonstrates. What is important is the warning implied to the reader who has just finished Pascual's neutral-toned narrative that, whatever a man's true motives may be, they remain unknowable. The caution is perhaps intended to advise us to infer more from what Pascual says than to believe at face value what is related as truth. The reader has no easy way of verifying the authenticity of the events chronicled and described. He must rely upon his ability to extract the true essence of Duarte's existence from the emotions the latter betrays in the course of his narrative. It is certainly the psychology of the man trapped by life that is uppermost in Cela's mind, not the mere anatomy of his behavior as that man describes it.

Criticism on *Pascual Duarte* is almost unanimous in viewing the novel as the history of a human being who has been trapped by his inescapable circumstance and forced by it into acts of atrocity, one of which occasions his imprisonment and execution. Such opinions range from those of Sherman Eoff, who believes that Pascual Duarte's tragedy is the result of his rejection by both family and society,[4] to the statements by Alonso Zamora Vicente, who discusses the novel as a study in the intensification of a single emotion, hate, which comes to engulf and to overwhelm the subject.[5] Speaking in much broader terms, Robert Kirsner has suggested, in passing, the possibility of seeing Pascual Duarte as an allegory of Spain.[6]

Consideration, moreover, must be given to Camilo José Cela. Writing for American students, he states explicitly:

> A Pascual Duarte le afeitaron la vida en el garrote y su arrepentimiento — que lo tuvo y bien firme — le libró de la gaita de andarse medio arrepintiendo a cada paso, como suele ser uso de burgueses, institucionalistas y timoratos, de todo o de casi todo lo que acontece. Pascual Duarte nunca supo a ciencia cierta por qué le apioló la justicia. Crímenes sí que hizo — y no pocos — pero Pascual Duarte, que se sentía incapaz de no matar, se murió ignorando las raras fuerzas que ajenas a su conciencia, le empujaban. A Pascual Duarte lo matamos entre todos porque resultaba demasiado incómodo mantenerlo vivo; la verdad es que no sabíamos qué hacer con él.[7]

Of course, Cela does not describe Pascual as innocent of the crimes attributed to him. Rather, society may be at fault for its inability to deal with men like Pascual, who, in the last analysis, are never fully aware of what they have done or why they have done it. The prologue that Cela has written to accompany the thirteenth Spanish edition indicates that the author has no desire to alter his position on the novel as it first appeared.[8]

Despite the near unanimity of opinion concerning the meaning of *Pascual Duarte*, David M. Feldman has a more optimistic attitude. He sees Pascual Duarte's behavior as a conscious human failing of which Duarte could have repented, but did not, until it was too late to save his life. His repentance is his autobiography, and his penance is his contrite and sorrowful recounting of his sins.[9]

Perhaps the most interesting interpretation offered to date is that of Mary Ann Beck. Stressing the structural ambiguity of the work, she succeeds in building a very convincing case for seeing the novel as a result of Cela's deliberate attempt to trick us into sympathizing with Pascual while providing signposts throughout the narrative to warn us of the irony, deceit, and falsehoods contained in the narrator's words:

> Si el lector no lee «con agudeza», se deja arrastrar por el persuasivo discurrir de Pascual sin examinar rigurosamente los hechos en sí. Se identifica con él y cae por tanto en la celada que le ha sido tendida por el autor. [. . .]Con esta técnica Cela exige mucho al lector; pero hay, claro es, ciertos recursos que le permitirán a éste discernir la veracidad de la interpretación de Pascual: juzgará la lógica de su discurrir, cojetará sus palabras con sus actos y verá los comentarios y las reacciones de los demás personajes.[10]

Although in her conclusions Miss Beck agrees with Feldman, her perceptive study of the structural ambiguity of the novel underlines, perhaps, the author's insistence that reality is deceptive, that there are no absolutes, and that the reader must form an opinion of Pascual Duarte more complex than just "good" or "bad."

A few of the structural possibilities and interpretational difficulties arising from the form in which Cela has chosen to present *Pascual Duarte* have already been mentioned. One basic question concerns the limitations and advantages of the autobiographical form. Often such an approach is considered extremely limited in perspective, since only that range of reality in contact with the unilateral narrator comes into view, and it is seen only in terms of his experience with it. What Pascual Duarte narrates is possible qua Pascual Duarte and only qua Pascual Duarte. The range of human experience is restricted enough for the reader to refuse to project that experience onto the larger plane of humanity in general. *Pascual Duarte* is essentially a novel of one man who is not necessarily a symbol of mankind. Therefore, the limitations of Cela's novel are limitations with respect to internal perspective.

One of the very real advantages of the autobiographical form, assuming that it derives from the author's desire to disappear behind his narrative, is that it permits the author great liberties without fear of recrimination on the basis of plausibility. With one internal point of reference for the narrative, it is difficult to dispute the facts as they are presented. This does not mean that, given two events and a conclusion, one cannot quarrel with the conclusion as it is drawn, but that singular events, incidents, and statements of sentiment have no second point of reference. The supporting levels of the novel refuse to provide this second point of reference.

An example of this liberty of perspective is Pascual's description of his mother. Pascual has many occasions to relate her life and habits in detail, concluding with a description of her animal fury as she is stabbed to death. Almost without exception Pascual's allusions to his mother are tinged with bitterness, resentment, revulsion, and hatred as he sees in her an incarnation of immorality and the adverse forces of the universe that pursue him. Since there is no other touchstone in the narrative against which Pascual's feelings might be measured, the reader has only the alternatives of believing that Pascual's descriptions of her are accurate or of doubting his sincerity. In the latter choice, little is to be gained by rejecting the only corpus of information available, Pascual's memoirs. In choosing the first alternative, the reader's trust is sorely repaid when he discovers in the concluding pages that the narrative leads up to Pascual's murder of his mother. In retrospect, his descriptions must be seen as an attempt to justify this act. In so adroitly hiding himself behind the façade of the novelistic edifice, the author has placed himself in a most advantageous position.

We may profitably ask at this point whether this type of organization is really more objective than the more heavy-handed third-person, omniscient approach common to the realist novel. Clearly it is, if objectivity is the opportunity to look at the narrative face to face without the bothersome presence of a detached or only secondarily involved narrator. If, on the other hand, objectivity refers to giving the reader the opportunity to examine and verify by comparison all of the facts at hand, then this type of organization is not objective. In reality, it could provide the author with a subtle way of forcing his message upon the reader. Indeed, herein lies a serious criticism of *Pascual Duarte*: that Cela has taken advantage of his form to describe a series of atrocities that can be accepted as plausible, but that the reader is unable to examine within a broad frame of reference. Given the manner in which we receive them, we can consider the atrocities only as forming a pathological casebook. Acts narrated by a person as seemingly unstable as Duarte are atypical of a large enough portion of humanity to put in serious doubt their validity as universal statements. Where exactly the line is to be drawn along the scale mounting toward these ultimate technical extremes depends upon one's conclusions as to the message of the novel. On the basis of Cela's own statement, Pascual Duarte is to be believed. But then Cela's own statement does not necessarily coincide with the conclusions drawn by the reader from the novel as it has been put together. Between the author's description of his work and the critic's description of it lies the value of the work as art.

Let us assume for the sake of argument that we may take at face value Pascual's declarations about himself and his family. What may one assume from the details chosen by Pascual Duarte? We know, for example, from the letter of transmittal and from the very existence of the memoirs, that Pascual Duarte is a man who has had occasion to think about his fate and has come to some conclusions as to his place in the universe. In short, Pascual has gained wisdom. It is a rough-hewn wisdom, but it is nevertheless the insight gained by an individual in the course of his basic struggle with life. Pascual's clinical retrospection and occasional introspection attest to the maturing process that has taken place since he experienced the incidents described.

With respect to the credibility of Pascual's wisdom, we must measure it in terms of the previously mentioned problems of perspective. In order to make Duarte's story more interesting and to engage our sympathies for a suffering and anguished soul, the author must endow Pascual with certain sentiments and emotions in agreement with the moral and ethical values of the reader. Despite the fact that Pascual is guilty of matricide, Cela has been careful to give him a notable sensitivity toward his fellow man. When Pascual recalls the sights and sounds and smells of the house where he was born, he does so with a certain melancholy that tempers the angry description of his parents. Pascual reveals his fondness for his sister, the only person in whom he finds solace. His brief but intense love for Lola, his first wife, and his early respect for Esperanza, his second wife, are calculated to raise him in the reader's esteem. When both women are unfaithful to him, the reader is ready to bestow his pity upon Pascual, who emerges as the victim. Duarte's recollections of his retarded brother Mario and the latter's grisly death are especially touching.

Pascual's sorrowful description of past acquaintances and painful experiences is in accord with the dominant note of confession and repentance that overshadows the events described. An extended stretch of narrative begins with Pascual's killing of the mare, and builds up through a description of his wanderings and homecoming and the subsequent death of his wife. This section of the novel is interrupted by an incident contemporary to Pascual's writing. Pascual relates the visit of the prison chaplain, who confesses and absolves Pascual while assuring him of the therapeutic value of writing the autobiography. In this way we are reminded of Pascual's essentially worthy intent as he narrates the vicissitudes of his life. The ensuing events are colored by the fresh reminder that they are related by the pen of a humbled and repentant sinner. Cela's irony is, of course, on a different level; it is not Pascual who is the sinner, but humanity in general and society in particular, an accusation that is supposedly too extensive for Pascual to grasp.[11]

But herein lies the problem for Cela. Danger inheres in attributing keen emotional sensitivity to the lowly Pascual Duarte. The reader is bound to ask himself at some point why Pascual is the victim of his family and why the others are his persecutors. With the exception of his sister, it is indeed "la familia de Pascual Duarte" that represents the forces closing in upon the hapless man. One explanation is obvious: It is Pascual Duarte who is writing and not, say, *El Estirao*, who might have had an equally moving tale to tell. This is not, however, a satisfactory explanation. If we search for an internal justification, some element that would explain Pascual's "difference," we must confess defeat. There is no way of proving that Pascual is not enhancing his own character.

The problem of credibility is compounded by the retrospective form the narrative assumes. Pascual Duarte as an individual with distinguishing emotional, moral, and ethical characteristics is contemporary to the recollection of his past. How much of the individual as a present entity accrues to the individual as a past entity or influences its interpretation is an important consideration. One wonders how much of Pascual Duarte's wisdom and maturity is the result of a gradual development throughout his life and how much is the result of the supposed repentance brought about by his imprisonment and death sentence. Again, these are things the reader cannot measure and therefore cannot criticize. Although Pascual's narrative would have us believe his wisdom developed gradually, we are completely free to attribute his emotional sensitivity to a new-found maturity that results from the critical self-evaluation undertaken during his imprisonment and culminates in his decision to write his autobiography of exculpation. Duarte certainly may be said to lack the fine insight necessary to distinguish his emotions as they may have been then from the manner in which he judges them now to have been. The reader may doubt the possibility of Pascual's feeling what he says he felt and yet doing what he says he did. But once he doubts, he must also assume the responsibility of evaluating and judging every one of the incidents related by Pascual. If this is the case, Cela has led the reader to an immediate confrontation with the material in question. The author need no longer show himself, and the reader-author-content relationship has been replaced with the desired direct contact between reader and content.

A few of the difficulties confronting the curious reader concern certain unexplained mysteries in the narrative. We wonder, for example, why Pascual kills his pet dog *La Chispa.* Since we are never told directly, all attempts at explanation are only conjecture. Given the character of Pascual's father as the former describes him, the reader is at a loss to explain the father's sudden tenderness for the new-born daughter Rosario, following his violent outburst at her birth. A more important unknown is represented by Pascual's final victim, don Jesús Gonzáles de la Riva, Conde de Torremejía, for whose murder Pascual is executed. Although mentioned several times in the narrative, he is never discussed. Pascual only vaguely refers to his murder with the ambiguous word "*rematar*" in the dedication. Any conclusion drawn as to the nature and importance of don Jesús is bound to color one's subsequent interpretation of events. Yet we are given no help externally by Cela nor internally by Pascual. The possibilities for interpretation this one element presents are to be seen in Zamora Vicente's extended and detailed analysis, which concludes by exonerating Pascual.[12]

Pertinent to the question of the validity of Pascual's emotions as he describes them are the problems of chronology and foreshadowing. It is important whether Pascual alters his chronology and his cause-and-effect relationship of events in order to highlight certain situations more effectively. Pascual's foreshadowing and alteration of chronology may be related to his attempts to deceive the reader and to show himself in a favorable light. By highlighting certain situations, the narrator in effect controls the impact of certain events on the reader. Such would not be the case if the format of a diary were employed. As near as can be determined, there is only one serious departure from the historical sequence of events in the narrative in Chapter One, which concludes with the shooting of the dog *La Chispa*. The second chapter begins with Pascual's description of the circumstances of his birth. Since *La Chispa* is alive in a later chapter when the mare is killed, one can only assume that the initial chapter is a prelude to what follows.

The other achronological aspects of Pascual's narrative are the interruptions in which Pascual speaks of himself in terms of his surroundings and feelings at the time of his writing, that is, while he is in jail. These interruptions serve a dual purpose. They provide the reader with the opportunity to learn what Pascual thinks of himself at that time and how he views himself in relation to the events which he is describing. By establishing two points of reference in time with respect to Pascual, the interruptions provide an opportunity to measure the awakening process as Pascual experiences it. However, this opportunity is severely modified by two dominant characteristics of the novel. On an internal level, our evaluation of the awakening process is very much conditioned by the narrative form. The underlying irony of the work, external to Duarte's narrative, when once grasped, serves further to hinder and condition such an evaluation. Pascual's interruptions may, of course, be simply attributed to a need for dramatic relief in the course of the narrative. But more important, and undisputedly so, they serve as reminders of the motivating impetus behind the memoirs.

Foreshadowing is another dominant literary device, and the use of it, supposedly by Pascual Duarte, raises some interesting questions. Duarte foreshadows the three most significant events of the novel: his wife's miscarriage and the killing of the mare, the murder of *El Estirao*, and the stabbing of his mother.

While the reader does not immediately anticipate Lola's miscarriage, there is an indication that the mare is going to create trouble at several points during the pair's short honeymoon, which ends with their return to the village, the mare's bolting, and the subsequent miscarriage. Foreshadowing occurs when Pascual describes their entry into Mérida. The mare starts and almost tumbles an old woman into the Guadiana. There is trouble over this incident, but it is quickly straightened out. To this trouble Pascual juxtaposes his first notice of an outward sign of Lola's pregnancy. Upon returning, he stops at the tavern and leaves Lola to find her way home after having referred briefly to her state. He has an altercation over his wife's virtue with one Zacarías, whom he seriously wounds, and upon returning home Pascual is informed of his wife's miscarriage. In his fury he attacks the mare.

When Pascual returns home after an absence of two years, his wife is pregnant by *El Estirao*. She appeals to her husband's mercy, but he forces her to reveal the identity of the father, and she dies in his arms, apparently of strangulation. Although she manages to extract a solemn promise from him that he will not avenge himself against *El Estirao*, the moment the latter appears on the scene, exuding the cockiness of a young buck, the reader senses what the outcome will be.

Since the murder of his mother is perhaps the most significant event of his autobiography, Pascual spends approximately one fourth of his narrative leading up to the stabbing that concludes his manuscript. This extended bit of foreshadowing begins with his release from prison after having served a three-year sentence for the murder of his wife's lover. Pascual laments the social system that returns him to his former way of life, supposedly opening the way for him to commit further acts of violence. He sees it as a *fatalidad* that he should slip back into the familiar rut of amoral chaos and violence:

> Da pena pensar que las pocas veces que en esta vida se me ocurrió no portarme demasiado mal, esa fatalidad, esa mala estrella que, como ya más atras le dije, parece como

complacerse en acompañarme, torció y dispuso las cosas de forma tal que la bondad no acabó para servir a mi alma para maldita la cosa. (p. 148)

Pascual's narrative begins to build up a somber background of inevitable and unavoidable forces in the universe. He describes the cemetery and its effect upon him, the heavy hand of Providence and the shadows that pursue him, and his awareness of "la sombra." The premonitions of the reader are confirmed with the rumination:

> La idea de la muerte llega siempre con paso de lobo, con andares de culebra, como todas las peores imaginaciones. Nunca de repente llegan las ideas que nos trastornan; lo repentino ahoga unos momentos, pero nos deja, al marchar, largos años de vida por delante. (p. 169)

Pascual's twisted and confused mind comes to realize the course his life is taking. There is one being who represents for him all of the elements that beset and persecute him: "No; no podía perdonarla porque me hubiera parido. Con echarme al mundo no me hizo ningún favor, absolutamente ninguno . . . No había tiempo que perder" (p. 174). Pascual's final words reveal the cathartic effect on him of his mother's death: "El campo estaba fresco y una sensación como de alivio me recorrió las venas . . . [. . .] Podía respirar . . ." (p. 176).

This abundant use of foreshadowing is not without its technical problems. It is possible to consider foreshadowing a subtle literary technique and to suspect the hand of the author upon the humble and rustic text of an unlettered criminal.[13] But it is not so simple as this. Pascual is in his fifties when he writes, and this older Pascual possesses much more sagacity and wisdom, if not intelligence, than does the Pascual about whom he writes. While it is difficult to justify Duarte's use of foreshadowing as a literary device, it may be the natural result of this newly-acquired wisdom.

Pascual is describing himself as he was and as he is. In retrospect, he is able to see a relationship between events that he probably would not have seen were he to have written his life as a day-to-day diary with descriptions contemporary to the events described. Pascual imposes a retrospective evaluation upon his life, and he is able, through his new-found insights, to see a relationship between the circumstances of his life and his acts of atrocity. However, a certain amount of fusion takes place between the past and the present in Pascual's narrative. As he becomes increasingly involved in the analysis of his state of mind before the murder of his mother, Duarte approaches a level of intensity in his descriptions that destroys the clinical detachment characteristic of his other chapters. Previously it was this detachment that helped to keep the past and present distinct.

The essential irony of *Pascual Duarte* is the very simple proposition that the individual, while he can tell us the events of his life, is not the best qualified to evaluate those events. Considered in the broader terms of the human and sociological context of the novel, Pascual's evaluation may indicate that he feels excessively guilty for his life. The reader might conclude from Pascual's descriptions of his environment that he could not have avoided the misfortunes which beset him and that his reactions are those of a simple man caught in a trap from which there is no escape. One of the frequent themes of Cela's later fiction is that man is cursed by an original sin, which explains his moral and ethical bankruptcy.[14] In *Pascual Duarte*, it is possible to see such an original-sin motif emerging. However, in view of the importance given by the author to the baseness of the family of man of which Duarte is a part, the latter is as much a victim of the perfidious influence of his fellow human beings as he is of his own sinful nature. In any case, if man is universally sinful, one man cannot be held responsible for his nature, which results from that sinfulness.

Pascual's docility following his violence and his repentance for his sins constitute the essential conflicts of his existence. Excepting the sense of torment leading up to the death of his mother, Pascual's only possible moment of lucidity is hidden behind the further mask of irony interposed by the author in the conflicting opinions of the priest and the guard. With Pascual's final moments obscured by these conflicting secondhand reports, it is difficult to discern if he experienced any comprehension before his execution. If one is to consider consistent the separation of the two levels of the narrator and of the author, the irony arising from the juxtaposition of these two levels is an ultimate refinement upon the central theme of the impossibility of knowing a man's motives and attests to the appropriateness of the formal vehicle chosen.

The foregoing discussion does not pretend to be a complete analysis of *Pascual Duarte* in terms of novelistic structure and technique. It is meant to serve as an introduction to certain basic problems of the novel as a coherent work of art. A fundamental assumption has been that the novel, at least today, cannot be merely the concatenation of amorphous occurrences, but is, rather, an attempt to interpret human experience through an ordering of what it relates. When an author such as Cela would avoid incurring sole responsibility for an ordering that assumes the author's superior point of view, the problems of structure are accordingly compounded and the question of the heavy but hidden hand of the author is raised. It is too early in this study to enter into an extended discussion of the author as *deus ex machina* in his fictional world. In the chapters to come, this factor will emerge as a constant in Cela's writings that implies a certain personal utilitarian concept of fiction. The novelistic world comes to constitute a private domain of human experience for the purposes of experimentation in the novel and of commentary upon the human situation.

2

Pabellón de reposo:

AN EXPERIMENT IN THE NOVEL OF PSYCHOLOGICAL INTROSPECTION

NO DOUBT inspired by the success of *La familia de Pascual Duarte,* Cela completed *Pabellón de reposo*[1] in Ávila in 1943, barely one year after the publication of his first novel. Although not issued in book form until 1944, *Pabellón de reposo* was serialized in *El Español* from March 13, 1943, to August 21, 1943. Paul Ilie, in his study, has done a capable job of analyzing *Pabellón de reposo*'s unusual structure in terms of possible meanings.[2] Therefore, this chapter deals less with the meaning of the novel as reflected in its structure than with *Pabellón de reposo* as a manifestation of Cela's growing interest in the novel as an experimental form of expression.[3] The analysis of *La familia de Pascual Duarte* assumed that Cela's first work employed a relatively traditional form; comments concerned the manner in which Cela dealt with the various technical aspects arising from that traditional form. In this and the subsequent chapters one basic assumption holds that Cela is constantly preoccupied with technical innovations in the novel.

Plot

Pabellón de reposo has little plot, and action is completely lacking. J. M. Castellet has summarized the novel as follows:

> *Pabellón de reposo* es una narración cuya acción discurre en el ambiente de un sanatorio antituberculoso. La novela

está dividida en dos partes, de siete capítulos cada una, y un intermedio. Los siete capítulos primeros relatan — en forma de fragmentos de diario, de monólogos interiores, de cartas o de diálogos — las impresiones, los deseos, las esperanzas de siete de los enfermos del sanatorio: el universitario del 52, la señorita del 37, el poeta del 14, la coqueta del 40, el enamorado del 11, la soñadora del 103 y el negociante del 2. Los siete capítulos de la segunda parte relatan los sufrimientos, las desilusiones, las desesperanzas y la muerte de esos mismos siete enfermos. Y el intermedio narra algunos de los aspectos de la vida de los que viven al margen de los enfermos: los médicos, las enfermeras, los cocineros, etc.[4]

Castellet's *etc.* is particularly significant, indicating the difficulties of describing the novel. One might add to Castellet's summary that there is a slight change in the outlook of the patients — from feeble hope to resignation — between the two parts. This change is the only "action." Of considerable importance, but generally overlooked, are the author's five interruptions in the course of the novel.

Formal and Structural Considerations

PABELLÓN DE REPOSO AS A NOVEL OF PSYCHOLOGICAL INTROSPECTION

A world of difference separates *La familia de Pascual Duarte* and Cela's second novel.[5] Aside from stylistic features, the two have in common very little in the way of technique and theme. The majority of the critics agree that *La familia de Pascual Duarte* is a social document. It is Pascual Duarte's life, seen in the light of his social circumstances, and the novel is oriented outward from the protagonist toward his external environment; what little we see of Duarte's inner being is always seen in terms of his particular relation to society.

On the other hand, *Pabellón de reposo* is oriented inward toward the examination of the inner beings of seven individuals from widely different backgrounds, all placed in the same situation and all faced with the same inevitable fate of premature death. The novel records their recognition of this fact and their reactions in the face of it. As such, it may be said to deal with permanent characteristics of the human soul. Life as it exists beyond the confines of the sanitarium is no longer important. Infrequently mentioned, the external world serves only to localize the seven even more vividly within their own restricted subcategory of the world. Although seen through the eyes of one individual, the world of *Pascual Duarte* is panoramic. Seen through seven pairs of eyes, the world of *Pabellón de reposo* is invariably the sanitarium, although a full physical description of the sanitarium is never given. The various patients refer to it in terms either of the atmosphere of the place or of the other patients with whom they come into brief contact. The author's interruptions provide more information concerning the *pabellón* than do the patients in the two hundred pages of the novel.

Pabellón de reposo is, then, the evocation of certain states of mind, certain emotional attitudes, and certain analytical insights as recorded by seven different, and introverted individuals. In its introspective approach, Cela's novel does not attempt to depict man's consciousness of his relation to society. The seven patients of the sanitarium have for the time being withdrawn from society, and, imprisoned by their sickness, they have begun to confront themselves. It is this naked portrayal of the individuals grappling with the unseen forces—in this case Death—that distinguishes *Pabellón de reposo* from other modes of Cela's fiction.[6]

FORMAL ELEMENTS

Pabellón de reposo is divided into two parts separated by an *Intermedio.*[7] Part One contains seven chapters that introduce seven different patients, alternating in sex, by means of written records they have left: No. 52 (*señor*), No. 37 (*señorita*), No. 14 (*señorito*), No. 40 (*señorita*), No. 11 (*señor*), No. 103 (*señorita*), No. 2 (*señor*). The written records are of three kinds: memoirs (Nos. 52, 14, 40, 103), letters (Nos. 11, 103, 2), and diaries (No. 37). In the case of the woman of 103, letters from the dead No. 73 are included in her memoirs. No.

11's letters are to his *amada*; No. 2 writes to his business manager. All seven texts are related in the first person.

In Part Two, the seven individuals are introduced again in the same order by means of the same written records. In Part One, each of the seven is presented without interruption or commentary on the part of the author. A *Nota del autor* interrupts the memoirs of No. 103. It contains no observations on this individual, however, and concerns the novel as a work in progress. Part Two is interrupted three times by the author in order to relate the deaths of Nos. 40, 11, and 103. The reader learns of the death of No. 37 from No. 52 (in Part Two) and of No. 14 from No. 37 (in Part One). In addition, each chapter in Part Two is concluded by a segment of a description of the funeral hearse. The entire description appears in Part One, recorded by No. 40 but attributed to No. 14. The segments, in order, are given in italics and are assembled to conclude Chapter VII of Part Two. The addition of the phrase, *Dentro, un hombre muerto*, informs the reader of the death of No. 2, whose letters make up the two Chapters VII. The novel is concluded by an *Epílogo*. Since its contents are parallel to Chapter I of Part One, we may attribute it to No. 52 (the only one who does not die in the course of the novel), thus giving him three representations as opposed to two for the other six patients. No. 52 is a sort of "internal author." He enjoys a point of view superior to that of the others, and his opening and closing remarks establish in part the theme of the novel. The "external author" is, of course, Cela, who appears as himself in the four interruptions, one *Intermedio*, and seven italicized tags that conclude the seven chapters of Part Two. For those who see *Pabellón de reposo* as a reflection of Cela's experiences in tuberculosis sanitariums, the impulse would be natural to relate Cela and No. 52.

Obviously, then, *Pabellón de reposo* has some sort of internal unity. There is a further tying together of the various sections of the novel by means of cross references between patients. Nos. 11 and 2 stand alone, neither mentioning each other nor mentioning the other patients. A certain amount of interdependence is revealed between the others: Nos. 37 and 52 are beginning to fall in love; Nos. 14 and 40 are mutually attracted; Nos. 37 and 40 depend on each other for companionship; Nos. 37 and 14 feel sorry for each other; No. 103 is vaguely attracted to No. 52, but is more involved with her memories of the dead No. 73. From these cross references in which the deaths of the others are mentioned, the reader knows that Part Two is later in time than Part One, but that in both parts the chronology runs from Chapter VII to Chapter I, thus:

VII-VI-V-IV-III-II-I—*Intermedio* and
VII-VI-V-IV-III-II-I—*Epílogo*

This seems to be the correct arrangement, since No. 37 relates in Part One the death of No. 14 in Chapter II. No. 14 occupies Chapter III and is alive for No. 40 in Chapter IV. In Part Two, No. 52 relates No. 37's death in Chapter I, but is still alive in Chapter II. Since there is a change of seasons recorded through the arrangement of the chapters as they stand, that is, I–VII, I–VII, one possible conclusion is that this is Cela's way of attempting the illusion of simultaneity. Although No. 37, obviously, cannot write after she is dead, it is possible to conclude that No. 52 is writing immediately upon learning of her death. In this way, the two parts represent two segments of time and two states of mind of the patients rather than the progression of time and the development of a state of mind that the reader might otherwise infer. The *Intermedio* accounts for any lapse of "natural" time, such as the lapse from August to November.

BALANCE AND PROPORTION AS AESTHETIC VALUES

The structure of *Pabellón de reposo* is unashamedly mechanistic. The reader finds himself hunting for interrelated elements that, rather than linking the characters as individuals one to another, serve to weave the sections of the novel together into one fabric. When such is the case with a work of art, we may speak of symmetry as an aesthetic quality sought by the artist.

Some of the overt structural attempts at symmetry have already been mentioned: the division of the novel into two parts, each with seven sections, and the alternation of male and female patients. A more covert patterning exists between a given section in one part and its companion section in the other part. For example, No. 37 is represented in both Part One and Part Two by consecutive entries from her diary; No. 2 is represented similarly by his correspondence to his business manager. Patterning of this sort tends to give a unity of impression for the various patients. Their identities and personalities remain stable and easily recognizable between the two parts. This patterning becomes important when we realize that we are viewing seven personalities at two different and relatively proximate periods of time. They remain quite the same people because there is little to upset their dreary equilibrium. Minute changes occur in their attitudes toward the state of their health in the direction of either despair or resignation, but these changes are more like new clothes in a new season rather than new feelings. Cela seems to find it necessary to reinforce any casual recognition of these changes through the use of the leitmotiv of the hearse, which builds up in intensity to the summation, where the whole passage is brought together again. Significantly, the summation occurs at the end of the chapter dealing with No. 2, who demonstrates the greatest change in attitude toward his hospitalization.

Another type of internal patterning, which is even more subtle but equally effective in giving cohesion to the various narrative units, is the use of stylistic parallels between the related chapters. They are of two types, organizational and syntactical. The organizational parallels are seen in the balance between the related chapters of the two parts. For example, No. 37, in Chapter II of Part One, is represented by twelve daily extracts from her diary, from Saturday the 12th to Wednesday the 23rd. In Chapter II of Part Two, she is represented again by twelve daily extracts from her diary, from Saturday the 5th to Wednesday the 16th. The only variation is that Sunday the 13th is missing, and, instead, there is a separate entry for the afternoon of Tuesday the 8th. No. 11, in Chapter V of Part One, is represented by three letters, one each for Monday, Tuesday, and Wednesday. In Part Two, Chapter V, No. 11 is seen again through three letters, one each for Monday, Tuesday, and Wednesday. Chapter VI of each part contains eight letters of No. 2, written from Sunday to Sunday. The other chapters, more random recollections and impressions in the nature of stream of consciousness, are not so rigidly identical.

The syntactic parallels are less noticeable and are of less importance to a discussion of the structure of the novel. These parallels occur when whole phrases appearing in Part One are repeated in the corresponding chapter in Part Two. No. 40 records in Part One: "el silencio es mayor, y el aburrimiento . . . ¡Ah, el aburrimiento es espantoso!" (p. 61). In Part Two she reaffirms: "El silencio es el mismo y el aburrimiento . . . ¡Ah, el aburrimiento es espantoso!" (p. 163). No. 11 asks, in Part One: "¿Por qué, Dios mío, no nos dices lo que hemos de durar . . . ?" (p. 81). In Part Two, he states: "Si Dios nos dijese lo que habíamos de durar . . ." (p. 181). No. 14 first writes: "El administrador me escribe diciendo que la sequía está arruinando la cosecha" (p. 57). He records later: "El administrador me escribe diciendo que la sequía ha arruinado la cosecha" (p. 159).

These are but a few examples; many more could be added. What is important is not so much the frequency of their occurrence, but the fact that they appear at all. This attention to such minute details of internal symmetry demonstrates Cela's growing interest in the novel as more than the casual-appearing sequence of events characteristic of more traditional forms of prose fiction. This attention to symmetry and structural patterning becomes a constant preoccupation in Cela's writings. In Cela's later novels, especially in *La catira*

(1955), such microstructural elements are obvious enough for Olga Prjevalinsky to have dedicated an entire study to them.[8]

The author has made an effort to call attention to his artifice. For Cela, the novel is no longer an unobtrusive vehicle, a mere expedient for commentary, but it has become as important as the commentary itself. *Pabellón de reposo* contains certain observations on life and man, made by seven patients in a tuberculosis sanitarium, as well as several rather direct statements by one who is undoubtedly the author himself. The novel also contains a commentary that is not made explicitly by the author nor by any of the patients. This commentary concerns the nature of the universe and the way in which the individual may see it as reflected in the structure of the novel. First, it seems apparent that Cela believes the novel may make a meaningful statement by presenting, at a given moment or moments, an objective cross-section of the minds of a randomly chosen group of people. Thus, the various balances and symmetries reflected in the proportioned selections, the attempts to construct simultaneity, and the mechanical alternation of representative patients are like vectors on a graph, converging at a certain point of common suffering.

Pabellón de reposo is the first, but by no means the last, of Cela's many attempts to order the chaos of the universe into a meaningful pattern. The novelist has accepted as a challenge the affirmation that the only meaningful patterns in the universe exist in the artist's mind. Although one may always question the extent of organization necessary in a novel, there is little doubt that such organization exists and that it exists for a very good purpose. The reader may criticize as unnecessary virtuosity the details with which Cela unites various sections of *Pabellón de reposo*. However, even the artist who considers art as a game usually has a serious reason that merits investigation.

Cela has on more than one occasion been accused of being glib and slick rather than profound,[9] and to a certain extent, this is true. His attitude derives from a sense of superiority—

natural to an artist from whom we demand insights not accorded to us — which in turn produces an ironical vision of mankind's attempts at living. Such irony is certainly evident in Cela's two great social panoramas, *La colmena* and *Tobogán de hambrientos*. Cela, as a novelist who must reduce what he sees to a manageable résumé, has found it convenient to believe in a superior perspective and the liberties it implies. Guillermo de Torre has observed,

> en Cela hay — más allá de su aparente sencillez de espejo — una reflexiva escogitación, un tamiz; en suma, elaboración artística. Ahora, donde plenamente hace diana nuestro novelista en trance de crítico es al escribir con enfoque más general: «Hay todo un mundo por encima y por debajo de lo natural y de lo real, que es también natural — puesto que en él no hay artificio — y real — ya que existe. Puestos a afirmar, declaríamos, sin reserva alguna, que identificamos lo natural con lo real, es más: que llamamos natural — o real — a todo lo que desde lo subreal llega hasta lo sobrenatural. Immerso en esa realidad — inquietante y misteriosa realidad — está el mundo literario de Solana, ese mundo que se posa ante sus ojos para que, con sus ojos, lo taladre y lo adivine».[10]

Cela's various artistic devices are attempts to localize and to define the reality that goes beyond what we observe. There is certainly a hierarchy based on insight and understanding among the various patients in *Pabellón de reposo*, a hierarchy that functions quite apart from the structural attempts at simultaneity and uniformity of impression. Cela, as the author in his own work and No. 52, his alter ego, enjoy the greatest vantage point. But No. 52 is by no means completely self-realizing, and Nos. 37, 14, 50, and 103 add to his characterization. No. 40 is the most realistically aware of her own predicament and of that of the others. No. 14 is the most introspective and sensitive, while No. 37 is the most naïve. No. 103, through her experiences with the dead No. 73, is the most all-inclusive in her feelings. Of the two who remain isolated, No. 11 is the most deluded of the seven, and No. 2 is the wisest. Although all seven are concerned with their disease and imminent deaths, the diversity of their attitudes, often reflected in small things, provides the necessary relief from Cela's overt structural elements. Yet, when the diverse attitudes are fitted together, they tend to support and to justify those very elements.

THE POSITION OF THE AUTHOR

The publication of *Pabellón de reposo* by installments in *El Español* provided Cela with the unique opportunity of intercalating into the novel reports on its progress and its reception by *El Español's* reading public. Cela as Camilo José Cela, author of *Pabellón de reposo*, appears five times in the course of the novel: once in the *Intermedio* between the two parts, once in Part One (in Chapter VI), and three times in Part Two (Chapters IV, V, VI).

Cela appears first in Chapter VI of Part One, well along in the development of the novel. *Nota del Autor, Antes de Seguir Más Adelante* (pp. 94–96) interrupts No. 103's description of the lettters from the now deceased No. 73. The *Nota* relates a request received from a doctor that the author cease publication of *Pabellón de reposo*, on the grounds that the revelation of the patients' emotional instability is not good for other tuberculosis patients. The novelist describes his initial distress and his subsequent decision to continue publication. There is no attempt to call the novel, the work of fiction, anything other than what it is. On the contrary – and observe the departure from the approach in *La familia de Pascual Duarte* – there is every effort to leave the impression that this novel is only a work of fiction:

> La carta del doctor A.M.S. me dejó perplejo. He estado una semana entera – de martes a martes – sin corregir pruebas, sin intercalar palabras donde el sentido no estaba muy claro, sin meter la tijera en los sitios que se me aflojaban farragosos o lentos, sin, en unas palabras, poner mano sobre mis cuartillas, pensando sólo en los párrafos, una y otra vez leídos y releídos, que mi amigo me dirigió. Jamás, en mi todavía corta carrera, pasé por momentos de mayor perplejidad, de espanto parecido, de análoga incertidumbre. (pp. 94–95)

This passage reveals a facetious effort to be explicit about the nature of *Pabellón de reposo*. Because the various sections of the novel purport to be letters and diaries from the pens of the patients themselves, the conflict between the autonomy of the author and the autonomy of his fictional realm is especially tense. Both the fiction and the author demand recognition as the truth: the fiction on the grounds that, internally, no one but No. 37 could have kept No. 37's private diary and only No. 2 knew his business well enough to write his correspondence; the author on the grounds that it is he who holds the pen, a fact he is more than willing to demonstrate. In a series of statements that would seem to invalidate this novel as Truth, Reality, Mankind in Microcosm, and other such abstractions that the novel has often pretended to be, Cela wryly observes:

> Que ningún enfermo, después de leída esta breve confesión de mi duda, se crea el ombligo del mundo. Que nadie piense que su desgracia es, realmente, ejemplar. Que no se identifique nadie con estos poco afortunados tipos de mi ficción.
>
> La señorita del 37 es una entelequia; la del 40, un vacío; la del 103, una sombra esfumándose. El enfermo del 14 es una mera apariencia; el del 52, un simulacro; el del 11, un fingimiento.
>
> Todo es artificio y traza – decía Don Quijote – de los malignos magos que me persiguen. ¿Por qué vosotros, buenos amigos, preoccupación de mi amable comunicante a quien tan poco voy a complacer, no pensáis en algo parecido? Id con vuestros malignos y mágicos perseguidores y no entorpezcáis mi marcha. Yo os prometo que tan pronto como piense que pudiera entorpecer la vuestra, me haré a un lado del camino. (p. 96)

The novel becomes a source of information, the characters and events being little more than stylized vehicles for commentary and judgment. What the novel is not, if we are to take Cela at his word, is a tight little imitation of life, inviting our identification and self-accommodation. Life may be all a stage, but, certainly, the stage is not all life.

The second break in the course of the novel is the *Intermedio* separating Part One from Part Two. This interlude is more extensive than the interruptions that are intercalated in the two parts. The *Intermedio* is divided into four parts: the report of a meeting of the sanitarium's board of directors, various descriptions of the sanitarium and characterizations of several staff members, the description of the patients gathered together in the lounge, and one Antón's concept of the relativity of time and events.

The report is a bit of background to the patients' self-analysis. Written from a third-person point of view, it includes several statistics given by the resident physician. His status report briefly mentions the very activity the novel pretends to represent: "Hemos observado también que casi todos aquellos clientes en quienes hemos visto esos trastornos [de desequilibrios nerviosos] se dedican a escribir con toda pasión sus diarios o sus memorias" (p. 114). This comment, the physical description of the *pabellón*, and the mention of certain staff members, all tend to support the fiction that such a sanitarium exists and that the letters, diaries, and memoirs that constitute the bulk of the novel really have come from the pens of certain of its inmates. The *Intermedio* does much to establish one of the basic themes of the novel—that a division exists in the world between the healthy and the sick.[11] This is accomplished by describing certain staff members and their sense of superiority toward the patients and by then presenting the suffering patients assembled in the lounge. To the narrator, the patients form a homogeneous group split only into the masochistic (*sufridoras*) and the sadistic (*mortificantes*). Looking in upon this scene, the narrator observes: "Un novelista tendría en aquel ambiente preciosos datos para sus libros" (p. 118). The author has again highlighted the irresolvable conflict between the author and fiction, first by going along with the fiction (the meeting, the status report, the descriptions, the staff), and then by seemingly invalidating that fiction when he refers ironically to his existence behind the novel as its prime mover.

Cela goes on to affirm his presence by referring ironically to his cousin Antón's philosophical theory that hypothesizes, "si corriésemos más que la luz podríamos ver la Historia" (p. 119). That is, we would move ahead in time if we could exceed the measuring-stick of relativity, the speed of light. The premises of the theory are open to question, but one approach used by novelists does exactly this: it starts with the present and searches back into the past to explain the present. This technique attempts to bring history within the limited span of the work of fiction and implies that such a rendering of history is both possible and desirable. Cela, nevertheless, concludes his summary of Antón's theory by seriously doubting both the possibility and the desirability of such an undertaking. The author reaffirms his intention to work only with simultaneous realities of the moment at hand. Referring to what might be derived from applying his cousin's theory to a previously described incident, Cela wonders: "Entre estas horas, lejanas, y aquellas otras, más próximas, en que paseaban su prohibido amor por carretera, pasaron cosas que, ¿para qué vamos a relatar?" (p. 120). With this expression of the novelist's lack of desire to explore the web of the past, Part Two begins immediately with seven more chapters of isolated present.

The next two interruptions, in Chapters IV and V, describe the deaths of Nos. 40 and 11. The first of these gives little insight into the author's relation to what he is writing or to his concept of the novel as fiction versus information. He tends to support the fiction by referring to No. 40's notebooks, which are taken from her and hidden when she is found delirious. If anything, the reporting of No. 40's delirium establishes a dual perspective, at least for what she has written in Part Two. We may either examine her notebooks and accept them at face value, or, with the superiority provided by the insight of the author, examine them again to prove to ourselves that No. 40's emotions are indeed unbalanced.

The second interruption in Part Two relates the death of No. 11 and records a letter from his *amada* declaring that she can no longer love him. The letter arrives too late. One passage may be read as a further affirmation by the author that he is going to view things as they are and not as they could be or would be under another set of circumstances: "Pero las cosas suceden como está escrito y no como nosotros quisiéramos que sucedieran, y el enamorado epistolario de nuestro amigo hemos de darlo truncado como quedó" (p. 181).

The third interruption in Part Two is much more extensive in nature than the other two, which are better considered as external observations upon the events contained in the two chapters concerned. The *Otra Nota del Autor Interrumpiendo la Narracion y Antes de Caminar ni un Solo Paso Más* (pp. 189–95) parallels the interruption in Part One. Both appear in Chapters VI, interrupting No. 103, and both are in italics, whereas the two other appearances of the author in Part Two are not. The content is also parallel; both relate an urgent plea from an outsider to discontinue publication. In the instance under discussion, the plea comes supposedly from an old friend of Cela's, himself a victim of tuberculosis. The particulars are unimportant, save to the extent that they correspond to Cela's biography.[12] Cela's justification for continuing his novel despite his friend's arguments is an explicit statement of the intent of his novel to capture a present and simultaneous set of realities, and no more:

> [. . .] y pienso que mi novela, lejos de producir un efecto deprimente, pudiera — de saberse leer con agudeza — hacer vibrar las cuerdas optimistas del lector, ya que los tipos presentados — los tuberculosos lo saben mejor que nadie — son, a más de entes ficticios, representantes de una manera de ser de hombre-tuberculoso o mujer-tuberculosa, de la que, como primera medida en quienes busquen la curación, habrá que escapar como del fuego. (p. 194)

Cela conceives of the novel as a vehicle for information, albeit an artistic and stylized vehicle. Although he is willing to accept the fictional artifice to the extent that all art is necessarily artifice, Cela is adamant, at least with regard to *Pabellón de reposo*, in believing that no one is deceived by the artifice, and therefore he refuses to force the issue. The basic premise is that the reality of the novel can only be a reality of the moment, captured and expressed in the form of fiction, and thus Cela's novel is a series of momentary realities that the structure of the novel attempts to make appear as simultaneous. Each character is seen for a few brief pages at two separate periods in time. No attempt is made to relate the periods either to the past or to the future, and no attempt is made to relate them to each other. They simply occur. The artistic canon supporting *Pabellón de reposo* holds that this is sufficient and perhaps all that is possible. In *Pabellón de reposo*, the fiction exists only when the author is ready to acknowledge its existence, and it disappears or becomes irrelevant when he chooses to talk about it as a figment of his imagination.[13]

A quite different aspect of the presence of Cela in his own work concerns the relation of *Pabellón de reposo* to the author's two periods in tuberculosis sanitariums. Cela has spoken out on the subject, stating that the novel *is* the result of his two experiences. He mentions the matter in the *Nota a la segunda edición*[14] and in the *Prólogo* to the sixth Spanish edition.[15] At the same time Cela hastens to add that he has used the personal experience simply as a suggestion.[16] This hardly would need saying if it were not that there are two "real" Camilo José Celas: one, a tuberculosis patient in 1931 and 1942 and the author of *Pabellón de reposo* as the result of his impressions; the other, the Cela who wrote *Pabellón de reposo* and published it in *El Español* over the protests of others. It is difficult to separate the external "real" Cela from the internal "real" Cela, and the confusion on the part of the critics between the novelist's personal experience and his fiction is understandable.[17]

3

Nuevas andanzas y desventuras de Lazarillo de Tormes:

THE REVITALIZATION OF A PROTOTYPE

STILL riding the wave of an early productivity, Cela finished *Nuevas andanzas y desventuras de Lazarillo de Tormes* in 1944.[1] His first period of fiction ended with this novel. Although in the subsequent years he published several other books—poetry, sketches, short stories—no new novels appeared until 1951.[2]

Given the fact that *Lazarillo* is a work of *imitatio*, it is not strange that the novel holds few technical and structural surprises. Two ways of approaching the novel are through a comparison with the model and through a discussion that stresses its prefigurement of Cela's later work, especially of the two social novels, *La colmena* and *Tobogán de hambrientos*. The present study will use both approaches but will emphasize the latter. Like *Pabellón de reposo*, *Lazarillo* is a minor work and a novel of apprenticeship. Unlike the former, it lacks the structural innovations and theoretical preoccupation that make the former so eminently discussable. Nevertheless, Cela's third novel constitutes an experiment in that its genesis involved using the form and orientation of a widely known prototype, the picaresque novel, and revitalizing it in terms of the thematics of the twentieth century. Such a revitalization involves the attitudes of the picaro toward his life and society and the necessity he feels for reviewing his career. Cela's novel is intimately concerned with whether or not a picaresque novel is possible in our age. The means by which he answers affirmatively constitute the main concern of the present chapter.

Plot

In the tradition of the picaresque novel, *Lazarillo* relates the adventures and experiences of an illegitimate child abandoned to the resources of his own wit. The novel is divided into nine *tratados*:

> Esta Obra se Divide en Nueve Tratados Que Son los Siguientes:
> PRIMERO Donde yo, Lázaro, cuento cómo pienso que vine al mundo y dónde y de quiénes.
> SEGUNDO Donde refiero cómo soy y hablo otras cosas del color y la estatura.
> TERCERO En el que oriento al lector para que conmigo pueda caminar el tiempo que caminé con el señor David, sin que le espanten humores de lagarto, ardores de alimaña ni olores de puerco.
> CUARTO Que trata de la paz que encontró mi alma paseando a orillas de los ríos, y habla también de las filosofias del penitente Felipe.
> QUINTO O del soledad; como ella accidentado y como ella breve y temeroso.
> SEXTO Que se refiere a la gimnasia como medio de ganarse la vida y perder la salud, y relata asimismo las extrañas costumbres del señor Pierre y la señorita Violette.
> SEPTIMO En cuyas planas escribo de la traza como acabó mi amistad con el poeta y hablo de mi corto y estéril aprendizaje del oficio de mancebo de botica.
> OCTAVO Levántate, Simeón, o el arte de echar las cartas.
> y NOVENO Donde relato cómo llegué a la Corte y con qué compañía, y pongo punto a esta primera parte del cuento de mi trotar. (pp. 23–24)

It is worth noting that the narrator of this work is inspired to his task through an acquaintance with the original work, acquired during his stay with the pharmacist.

Formal and Structural Considerations

FORMAL ELEMENTS

The arrangement of *Lazarillo* shows no outstanding characteristics. Neither internal patterning nor linear progression of incidents toward a high point or climax occur in the development of the narrative. The work is enclosed by the two very natural and simple events, Lazarillo's birth and his entrance into the military. Besides the nine *tratados* dealing with his youth and adolescence, the narrator includes a *Dedicatoria* and an *Epílogo*. There is no intrusion of Camilo José Cela either as an interested party or as the author. Following the tradition of the picaresque novel, the author gives the word completely to the narrator. The author appears once, as the publisher in the concluding *Nota del editor*, which relates his interview with the aged Lázaro in the hospital of San Juan de Dios in Madrid concerning the sequel to Lázaro's autobiography, promised in the *Dedicatoria*. Unfortunately, none exists, nor is there any hope that it will ever appear. Thus, the events as they stand represent all that is available and constitute a partial, but in itself complete, whole.

There is no particular significance in the organization of the *tratados*.[3] Six represent actual masters and three represent transitions (the second, a self-portrait; the fifth, a nightmare; the ninth, Lázaro's recruitment and the end of his story). His masters are, in order, several shepherds (I), three musicians (III), Felipe, the penitent (IV), Pierre, the gymnast and his company (VI), don Roque, the pharmacist (VII), Tía Librada, the Celestinesque woman-of-all-trades (VIII). With the exception of *Tratados* VI and VII, which are connected by Lázaro's stay with the poet don Federico, whose charity he enjoys and whom he does not "serve," the various divisions stand autonomous. The arrangement of the masters, their occupations, and their characters, betrays no line of internal development. Their various persons and Lázaro's various experiences with them represent no movement toward an increased awareness or toward awakening on the part of the narrator.

The lack of a narrative crescendo developing during the course of the novel eliminates a problem sometimes created by the autobiographical form. Since nothing outstanding happens to Lázaro, the manner in which his life is reported is of little consequence. The choice of the point of view appears to derive more from the tradition of the picaresque novel than from the orientation of the present novel.

COMPARISON OF THE PROTOTYPE AND THE "IMITATION"

One of the classic characteristics of the picaresque novel is the theme of initiation into the economic and social hardships of the life of the lower classes. The novel usually ends with the narrator aware of the fact that only he can do something about his situation in life. The picaresque novels are the precursors of the contemporary novels of adolescence employing the theme of the youth's initiation into life. Although the concept of the life into which the initiation leads has changed with the changing preoccupations of mankind, a permanent characteristic is the cessation of the sequence of events – the stages of initiation – once a sufficient wisdom and maturity have been attained, usually coupled with a sharp sense of realization. The sequence of events may be said to contain a built-in climax that definitely brings the narrative to a close.[4]

One of the fundamental differences between the two *Lazarillos* is the degree to which the sequence of events in each book forms a complete unit. The original *Lazarillo de Tormes* ends with the narrator's acquiring a certain station in life, a humble but secure bit of respectability. This step up the social scale allows him to look upon his past life and former acquaintances with a certain superiority. The original Lázaro recalls a closed unit of events, a period in his life above which he has permanently risen. Since the sequence of events is clearly delineated and fixed in the past, Lázaro is able to examine it with some degree of objectivity and to comment upon it with detachment. He recognizes it as the formative period for his personality and sees it as his awakening to the hardships of life and his initiation into the basic creatural struggle for survival.

The conclusion of Cela's novel, on the other hand, is not independent of the sequence of events it reports. The modern

Lázaro's narrative ends with his draft into the military. Although this is certainly a common turning point in a contemporary young man's life, it does not necessarily coincide with his awakening and initiation into life. Instead of gaining insight and accepting responsibility, Lázaro speaks of losing his freedom:

> ¡Allí acabo mi libertad! Madrid, donde me las prometía tan felices, me metió en el cuartel, y en él, aunque a los dos meses escasos me sacó de asistente el teniente Díaz, me encontraba al principio como pienso que han de encontrarse los mirlos y los jilgueros al llegar a la jaula. (pp. 227–28)

The effect is to consider the present less favorable than the past, an attitude that is the complete reverse of the one implied by the earlier novel. Thus, the sequence of events in *Lazarillo* does not come to a significant and definitive close. While it is true that Lázaro has ceased to be a vagabond for the time being, there is nothing to prevent him from returning to his wanderings at some time in the future; he experiences no break with the past, no rising above it, and no new-found maturity of perspective. *Lazarillo* is an open unit, and it is not surprising that the narrator refers to it as the first of several installments of his life's story. That there are no follow-ups to Lázaro's narrative is, of course, an entirely external consideration.

The difference between the sequence of events in the two novels holds true also for the nature of events. In the original *Lazarillo de Tormes* the various events serve to highlight a final set of circumstances and at the same time give a panoramic description of a particular segment of sixteenth-century Spanish society. As segments of a particularly significant whole, the individual events, built around Lázaro's six masters, are best considered as exempla. The masters are types that reflect established sectors of Spanish society—the familiar figures of the vagrant and mendacious blind man, the clergyman, the destitute squire, the vendor of papal bulls. From each Lázaro learns a little more about the circumstances of life and the conditions with which he must deal simply to stay alive. It is a learning process that eventually leads toward Lázaro's ability to raise himself above his circumstance and to cope knowingly with it.

In Cela's *Lazarillo*, since the events lead up to no conclusive finale, the nature of Lázaro's several experiences and the character of his several masters tend to be miscellaneous. According to Marguerite C. Rand, the basic motivating force of the original Lázaro, hunger, is completely lacking in Cela's hero. The twentieth-century Lázaro faces the reality of his social context:

> This new Lazarillo lives not only in a world of masters but in a world of nature of which he is at times very much aware. This is a story of Lazarillo and his "circunstancia," of which the lands and villages through which he travels are also an essential part. Thus, one aspect of this novel, completely absent in its predecessor, is the portrayal of nature and landscape, which gives to the whole an illusion of reality, the reality of Spain and particularly of Castile, as sought, likewise, by the writers of '98 in this era. . . . This Lazarillo has a modern sensitivity to Nature. He sees the world about him, and his comments on his "circunstancia" reveal a twentieth-century preoccupation for Spain. He is aware of life's reality and also its mediocrity and absurdity and will not be subject to it. In his desire for "lo maravilloso," he weaves about it fantastic tales which form an artistic balance to his harsh comments on the real Spanish villagers, villages, and landscapes.[5]

Miss Rand's point is well taken that *Lazarillo* tends to make certain statements concerning the individual as an ethical being, his pretense, and his reality. Toward this end, the author uses expertly a technique of combined reality and fantasy.[6] Cela's intent is to evoke certain universal characteristics of the human personality rather than to give a complete vision of one segment of society. Therefore, *Lazarillo* incorporates a series of events that have no necessary interrelation and that do not constitute a unified whole. The variety of the sixteenth-century Lázaro's masters derives from the necessity for completeness in the evocation of types; the variety of the modern Lázaro's masters originates in a desire to give as much empirical evidence as possible about the essential traits of the human personality. The former are necessarily types, while the latter, although including some types (the shepherds, the pharmacist), are individual cases. José María de Cossío comes to this conclusion in his *Prólogo* to our edition:

> Estos personajes de Cela no representan, como podían representar los puestos en pie por los viejos novelistas picarescos, clases sociales, estratos definidos y operantes de la vida española. Son casos y no tipos. Son caracteres singulares, más próximos en algunos casos a la realidad que sus antepasados, pero por excepcionales más aptos para la complacencia literaria que para la lección moral, o inmoral, aplicable e inmediata. (p. 19)

The point of view in *Lazarillo* implies the problems discussed in connection with the position of the author in *La familia de Pascual Duarte,* although the difficulty of structural organization and the interpretation of the novel in terms of it are not so great. Any discussion of *Pascual Duarte* is complicated by the layer of irony surrounding the central narrative, an irony created by the contrast between the first-person narrative by Duarte and the external information derived from other sources. However, there is no such irony in *Lazarillo*, since there is no juxtaposition of different points of view. Cela appears only once at the end of the narrative in the *Nota del editor* simply to explain the connection between the writing of Lázaro's autobiography and its publication. It is an appearance that serves to give an external verisimilitude and reality to the autobiography rather than to contradict and ironize it. Instead of ascribing the autobiographical form to an attempt at irony, the reader accepts it as part of the tradition of the picaresque novel. It is better to recognize the author as the narrator and to speak in terms of the perspective enjoyed by the latter.

The original and the modern *Lazarillo* differ also in the

perspective of the narrator. The first Lázaro's perspective is narrow, in keeping with his limited station in life and his contact with a limited stratum of society. The sixteenth-century work is restricted in its point of view because of the peculiarity of its thematic intent. In order to make its point, the novel distorts and exaggerates reality. The result is a work that is antirealistic because of the very limited contact the narrator-protagonist has had with life. Lazarillo's low birth and his circumstantial adverse fortune have brought him in contact with only the dregs and the near-dregs of society. Externally, the implication is that the author is interested only in a limited segment of society that is consistently portrayed unfavorably. The message of the picaresque novel must be measured in terms of the exaggerated and involved portrayal of one segment of society. And its message is clear with respect to the immorality that segment of society breeds in its struggle for survival.

To a certain extent the same is true of Cela's work. Being within the tradition of the picaresque novel, it is understood that the author intends to comment in the same way upon mankind. However, the greatest difference between the modern work and the prototype is that the latter is not restricted to a defined sphere of society. There is no thematic limitation on the individuals with whom the modern Lázaro comes in contact; the only restriction placed upon them arises from the geographic limitations of his wanderings.

Another point of departure from the prototype is that Cela's Lázaro is a willful rather than an accidental vagabond. He is a man on the move who seeks his masters and, growing disillusioned, dissatisfied, and disgusted with one, moves on in search of another. Lázaro is the *homo viator* who goes out to meet life on its own highways in the tradition of the travelers in the works of Dante, Bunyan, Gracián, and Cervantes. Lázaro finds his fellow moderns in the American novel of more notoriety but less quality, Kerouac's *On the Road*. It is therefore not surprising that Paul Ilie is able to see a relationship between *Lazarillo* and Cela's travelogs.[7]

Lázaro serves as a source of information concerning human experience. While the sixteenth-century Lázaro is also a source of information, his information is more in terms of his own former social circumstance, from which he has escaped and on which he is looking back. In Cela's work, Lázaro's experience with his various masters is not a social but a human one. When he changes masters, it is not because of hunger or poor accommodations, but because of disgust and disillusionment with them as human beings. The few with whom he is happy either die (Felipe), get bilked because of him (don Federico), or disappear (Tía Librada).

When Lázaro, the *homo viator*, ends his travels in the *cuartel* in Madrid, his narrative also ends, since it is based upon those travels in its reconstruction of his human experience. Lázaro does not hesitate to recognize their importance:

> Cuando al cabo del tiempo me licenciaron, tenía todo: una documentación, una cartilla, un certificado de buena conducta . . . Lo único que me faltaba eran las ganas de seguir caminando sin ton ni son por los empolvados caminos, las frescas laderas de las montañas y las rumorosas orillas de los ríos.
>
> Me sentí viejo (¡entonces, Dios mío!) por vez primera en mi vida, y me encontré en la calle otra vez con el cielo encima y la tierra debajo.
>
> Los primeros días los pasé con los cuartos que me dió un ama de cría que conocí de soldado. Después . . . Después empezó la segunda parte de mi vida. Pasé por momentos buenos y por instantes malos; conocí días felices y semanas desgraciadas; gocé la buena salud y padecí el hambre aún mejor. . . , y llegué, paso a pasito, a lo que hoy soy.
>
> Contar el camino, ¿para qué? Fué la espinosa senda de todos quienes conocí. . . . (p. 228)

In his own mind, Lázaro's early wanderings and his experiences prefigure the essence of his life as a whole. Therefore, his earlier experiences are indicative of the total experience of his life. Feeling that the story of the rest of his life would add nothing new, he declines to deal with it: "[. . .] nos respondió que [la segunda parte] en su cabeza seguía, porque había pensado que así había de ser mejor por aquello de que nunca segundas partes fueron buenas. [. . .] Quizá Lázaro tuviera razón" (p. 235). Cela's work also differs fundamentally in this way from the older one, since the earlier experiences of the sixteenth-century hero do not prefigure the relatively comfortable existence in his new-found security.

THE VALIDITY OF CELA'S EXPERIMENT

Some critics have seen *Lazarillo* as little more than an imitation of the original *Lazarillo de Tormes*.[8] Such is the case with J. M. Castellet: "Cela se ciñó demasiado a las formas primitivas y cayó en el error de creer que una simple traslación de la anécdota a nuestros días bastaba para darle modernidad a la novela."[9]

Robert Kirsner, on the other hand, affirms Lazarillo's autonomy in a rather roundabout way when he writes:

> It is the contemporaneity of his essential make-up, rather than his literary historicity, that sustains Lázaro's characterization of himself and his environment. It is further this sense of isochronism in events that lends force to the grotesqueness of Lázaro's peregrinatory existence. The revulsion that Lázaro inspires — and he is the most obnoxious of Cela's characters — occurs because his experiences are propinquous to the present, if not concurrent with it. More than his literary «grandfather» of the 16th century, this modern rogue seeks to encompass social totality, to be a crude representation of prevailing values and ideals. His birth as a literary character occurs after he has reflected on his sense of symbolic «open» reality.[10]

Zamora Vicente's evaluation is one of the few that mention the obvious merits of Cela's novel:

> Para muchos, la vuelta al mito es, sin más, una torpe — o mañosa — recreación arqueológica. El autor escoge del mito los rasgos que le parecen más sobresalientes (los que le parecen a él, no los que realmente tiene el héroe antiguo) y los vuelve a poner en circulación, generalmente en un tono falaz, arcaizante. Abundan los ejemplos. Para otros,

y esto me parece lo único verdadero, y Camilo José Cela está en esta línea, volver al mito no es hacer el viaje a través de siglos y acaeceres, sino traer el mito a hoy, reactualizarlo, intentar ver aquí y ahora lo que de permanente y palpitante encierra la lección del clásico. Los clásicos no son clásicos, decía Ortega, más que para ellos mismos. Hagamos nosotros otro clasicismo, el nuestro, procurando aprovechar su experencia. Y esto es lo que ha intentado Camilo José Cela en el *Nuevo Lazarillo*.[11]

In addition to these comments, on the basis of the comparisons in the foregoing section, it is necessary to discard those critical statements which consider Cela's novel as little more than a twentieth-century updating of the picaresque motive. *Lazarillo* does not merely translate the events, individuals, and conclusions of the Renaissance masterpiece into modern terms; despite Lázaro's own naïve belief, hardly justified by his biography, that he is the direct descendant of the original Lázaro de Tormes, he is more than a dressing-up of the earlier antihero in the trappings of the "modern man in search of his social identification." Admittedly, *Lazarillo* corresponds in many respects to the prototype of the picaresque novel. However, within the traditional framework, Cela has gone far beyond giving a portrait of a limited sector of society to concentrate his attention on the behavior of man as an ethical being. If this is true, *Lazarillo* must not be judged in terms of the degree to which it approximates a modern vision of the sectors of society dealt with in the earlier work, but must be left to stand on its own merits as a novel typically contemporary and typically Cela. Discounting his sense of a necessity to see Cela's novel as an imitation, I agree wholeheartedly with Alborg's estimation:

La tercera andadura de Camilo José Cela escogía nuevos caminos, esta vez los fértiles y bien acreditados de nuestra vieja picaresca, de la que el libro — *Nuevas andanzas y desventuras de Lazarillo de Tormes* — es un remedo afortunado. Si hubiera sido escrito allá por los años de su homónimo o por los más erizados del Buscón, sería un libro famoso, porque ni en buena prosa ni en desdichas y picardías cede un ápice a sus congéneres.[12]

Lázaro, as *homo viator*, serves to link a series of narratives concerning the behavior of man. Unlike the portrayal of man's emotions in *Pabellón de reposo*, a portrayal in terms of the inner being of man, *Lazarillo* examines man in his "natural habitat" as Lázaro finds him in his wanderings. The range of types and individuals is necessarily restricted because of the nature of the narrative and the relative brevity of the novel. But there is little doubt that it is society as an ethical group that concerns Cela in this work, and the validity of his experiment must be seen in these terms. *Lazarillo* demonstrates a new aspect of Cela's concern with the novel as a source of information concerning man and mankind and indicates a new direction taken at this time by Cela's fiction toward a panoramic vision of society as interaction. Although *Lazarillo* lacks the notoriety of *La familia de Pascual Duarte* and the technical innovations of *Pabellón de reposo*, it is significant both as an excellent novel and as an experiment. Cela's novel is an effort to give a broad overview of man functioning within the ethical web of society. Men unwittingly reveal themselves to Lázaro, forgetting that the orphaned ragamuffin will also become a man and, as a man, will understand their motives and judge them accordingly. *Lazarillo* is limited in its scope, although it succeeds in defining well its vision of mankind. With this novel, Cela's apprenticeship period is closed, having provided him with the orientation and the techniques necessary for him to write his most highly esteemed work, *La colmena*.

4

La colmena:

THE READAPTATION OF THE NOVEL AS A VISION OF SOCIETY

CELA's fourth novel, *La colmena,*[1] was published in Buenos Aires in 1951. *La colmena* joined *La familia de Pascual Duarte* to extend Cela's fame abroad and to establish him as Spain's leading resident novelist. The importance of *La colmena* is due in part to its documentary nature, which creates as bleak a picture of Spanish society after the Civil War as *Pascual Duarte* gives for the years prior to that conflict. But of more interest to literary critics has been the structure of the novel. *La colmena* represents a radical departure not only in Cela's fiction, but in the Spanish novel as well. In the preceding chapter of this study, it was shown that *Nuevas andanzas y desventuras de Lazarillo de Tormes* reveals an orientation for the novel that leads up to the extensive panorama of society given by *La colmena.* This chapter undertakes to discuss the characteristics and the structure of that neorealist orientation.

Plot

It is increasingly difficult, as Cela's career unfolds, to speak of plot in his novels. If the theory is correct that Cela has been developing the novel into a stylized source of information concerning states of the individual, seen both in terms of himself and in terms of society, such a plotless world is not difficult to explain. Although *La colmena* is one of Cela's longest novels, it encompasses the shortest span of time. Various incidents, some interrelated and some isolated, in the lives of over three hundred people during less than forty-eight hours in the year 1942 make up the six chapters of the novel. A *Final*, a few days later in time, centers on one incident in the life of one individual, Martín Marco, as it is seen by others linked to him throughout the major part of the novel. Although there are about three hundred identifiable individuals, Marco ostensibly is of primary interest, since it is he who unifies several parts of the work. Along with Marco there are perhaps twenty to twenty-five other personalities who stand out enough to be labeled as principal or supporting characters. The six chapters and the *Final* are composed of 185 separate narrative units, each one usually with a locale and a group of characters distinct from the two that flank it. Although the novel is equipped with a *Censo de Personajes*, listing the various appearances of a given character and giving a brief descriptive quotation for purposes of identification, the reader is well advised to keep a tally sheet if he wishes to follow the various threads of action accurately.

Nevertheless, action is not the principal concern of the novel, an observation substantiated by the fact that action is so thoroughly fragmented. The only extraordinary happening is the incident mentioned in the *Final*. But, with Marco, the reader never learns exactly what has happened, and why the police want to question Marco remains a mystery. More than narration, *La colmena* is concerned with the vast canvas of Madrid society created through the individual and collective interactions of the many characters of the novel.

Formal and Structural Considerations

FORMAL ELEMENTS

Despite Paul Ilie's extended remarks,[2] much remains to be said concerning the structure of *La colmena*. Much of what has been said tends to be repetitive and undirected in its approach to the basic problems of the novel. In dealing with *La colmena*, critics usually find it necessary to speak of Dos

Passos' *Manhattan Transfer* or Baroja's novels, particularly of *La lucha por la vida*, of the influence of naturalism, of camera or cinematographic technique. Of course, to a certain extent these literary comparisons and technical similes are helpful, but, as does any comparison, they detract from the examination of the work itself; influence studies rarely clarify either the content or the structure of the work in question. It would seem that a direct discussion of the technical problems raised by a work of art cannot profitably be replaced by an approach through comparison and simile. One alternative approach to the novel is to discuss the ways in which Cela has attempted to put into effect his basic premises concerning the novel.[3] Of particular interest are the organization of the work and the nature of events. The following discussion will attempt to show how the internal structure of *La colmena* is related to Cela's program for the novel.

La colmena is a complex novel when seen in terms of its superstructure.[4] It is divided into seven parts, Chapters I–VI and the *Final*. The action of the chapters represents events that take place during two days; the events of the *Final* take place one morning a few days later. According to the *Censo de Personajes* compiled by one José Manuel Caballero Bonald, there are 296 imaginary characters created by Cela, and 50 historical or authentic individuals are mentioned in the course of the novel as well. It is necessary to examine in detail the several divisions of the novel in order to appreciate how Cela puts into effect his novelistic principles.[5]

Chapter I relates the events of the afternoon and early evening of the first day. The locale for all but one of the narrative units (I.33, 62) is doña Rosa's café in Madrid. Here a wide range of individuals are presented, all interrelated on the basis of their varying degrees of attachment to the café. Although not identified by name at first, the main character of the novel is presented midway in the chapter (I.20, 44). Martín Marco, unable to pay for his order and expelled from the café, has all eyes turned upon him, thus bringing together briefly the interests of the *tertulianos*. Although doña Rosa dominates the chapter as the overwhelming proprietress of the café, she serves in this first chapter as a springboard for Marco's introduction through her hardheartedness in having him thrown out.

Chapter II deals with the evening of the same day. The first narrative unit (II.1, 83) re-enacts the expulsion from the café from Martín's point of view and in this way establishes him as the dominant figure of Chapter II. He appears several times throughout the first two thirds of the chapter (to II.29, 118). The last third is devoted to the events surrounding the discovery of the murder victim, doña Margot (II.31, 120, and II.38, 128). Marco is not mentioned in connection with the murder. But the fact that he is the central figure of the novel, that the murder is the only real event of the novel, and that in the *Final* Marco is wanted by the police for questioning tend to point to a strong link here.

Chapter III jumps ahead to the evening of the second day to portray scenes in the café and elsewhere. Martín appears briefly only three times.

Chapter IV moves back to the night of the first day and consists chiefly of night scenes. Martín dominates this chapter, and it closes with him in the arms of a prostitute, where he has sought refuge from the winter cold.

Chapter V tells of the evening of the second day and follows Chapter III in time. Don Roque and his family are highlighted. Unlike the other six divisions of the novel, this one is not internally chronological. Events of several days previous are seen in flashbacks. Martín appears only twice.

Chapter VI takes place on the morning of the second day, thus following Chapter IV and preceding Chapter III in time. It is a short chapter and surprises several by-now familiar characters in the process of facing the new day. Martín is prominent among them.

The *Final* concentrates on Martín a few days later as he takes a morning stroll. The newspaper under his arm contains the yet-unread notice of the warrant out for his detention. Cela alternates accounts of Marco's stroll with sketches portraying the reaction of his friends and relatives to the notice that they read and comment upon with alarm.

SEQUENCE OF EVENTS

Cela does not present the events of his novel in a chronological order. If we were to arrange the chapters to correspond with the sequence of events, we would have to read them I–II–IV–VI–III–V–*Final.* The author interrupts several natural chains of events in rearranging the chronology of his novel and follows several narrative threads throughout the two days encompassed by *La colmena.* Since the several chapters are not isolated entities but record happenings that are interrelated as well as pertinent to the surrounding chapters, the author needs a good reason to break the narrative in this manner. One explanation is that Cela uses fragmentation of the chronology of his novel as a means to create an illusion of simultaneity, an effect he attempted to achieve in *Pabellón de reposo.* In the earlier novel, Cela was interested in creating the illusion of several states of emotion occurring and being recorded at the same time. Two periods of time are established, and the only "movement" of the novel is the shift in emotions between the two points in time. Such a procedure corresponds to a belief expressed by the author at that time that the novel cannot go beyond the creation of static states of mind. The novel would consist of no more than the juxtaposition of several such static states.

Cela's concept of the novel has developed further in *La colmena.* Although he continues to believe that a minute sampling of human activity constitutes sufficient evidence for a broad statement concerning the human situation, Cela is now far more willing to concede the necessity of seeing man acting in his circumstances than he was in *Pabellón de reposo.* The sequential order of events and the manner of achieving simultaneity in *La colmena* correspond to this modified attitude toward the range of possibilities of the novel.

The first characteristic of Cela's ordering that comes to mind is an attempt to give the novel the appearance of a hermetic unit. Discounting the *Final*, by returning in Chapter VI to a point in time previous to other parts of the novel, Cela creates the illusion of a closed world to the extent that we are able to predict the future on the basis of what happens in this last chapter. Chapter VI is the morning of the second day. The reader has already seen what is to happen during the afternoon and the evening of the second day, in Chapters III and V. Thus, the novel can end on no new note but can only lead the reader back to previously related events. The result is a period of time in the lives of certain individuals that is complete in itself and without any positive relation to the future. Again, as in *Pabellón de reposo*, there is no picture of man *becoming* in his emotional and psychological development. Rather, we see man as he *is*. The difference between the one novel as a description in terms of an internal set of relationships and the other as a description of external and social interactions concerns the differences between two modes of the novel.

The *Final* takes place several days after the two days covered by the bulk of the novel. The content is single-minded and bears no discernible relation to the body of the novel other than its use of already familiar characters. Although the reader connects Martín Marco with doña Margot's murder, he cannot be sure of his judgment, and Cela prefers not to clarify the issue. In this way, the *Final* stands structurally as a unit entirely separate from the rest of the novel. It is open in that it points towards a future sequence of events (specifically, Martín's arrest), the outcome of which we do not know and cannot predict. It may be said to form the beginning of another series of happenings that, if given, would resemble those in the chapters of the novel as they stand. Cela seems to indicate that the events of the world and the actions of man in his day-to-day routine are essentially repetitive. Although the *Final* opens the way for a new chain of events not implied in the closed units of Chapters I through VI, there is no need for us to think that the new happenings will reveal any more about mankind than what has already been said. True, the circumstances of life are surprising and uncertain. But a random sampling of them, according to Cela's novel, is a sufficient exegesis of man's behavior in these circumstances.

Cela's abrupt reopening of the novel, after having so effectively—albeit artificially—closed it, seems to be a bit of perverse teasing. Certainly, the reader who imagines the novel as ideally a suspenseful adventure story will be frustrated and disappointed. Cela's novel is not designed to titillate the reader's sense of the mystery of fate and the wonder of living the unknown. In fact, the attempt is to approach the known, the given qualities of life, as closely as possible; the unknown is but variation on an ancient theme. Of necessity, therefore, Cela's novel brings little information concerning life not readily available to the perceptive and sensitive observer of society. The rationale for such a novel is that most readers are not perceptive and sensitive observers of life and society.

Although *La colmena* aims at relative simultaneity for events in the lives of three hundred individuals, it does not have the rigid insistence upon the present of *Pabellón de reposo.* The latter has little recourse to the past, and none at all to the future of the seven individuals concerned, unless it is ever-present death. On the other hand, *La colmena* freely makes use of past events, often indulging in a complete biographical sketch of a particular character. Although Cela feels free at any point to interrupt the course of action in order to sketch in rapidly and often humorously the antecedents of a person, it is only in Chapter V that past events are brought in to explain or clarify present happenings. Chapter V is devoted to the family of don Roque Moisés Vázquez, brother-in-law to doña Rosa, proprietress of the café that is a backdrop for much of the novel. The various events relative to his love affair and to that of his daughter Julia extend beyond the earliest limit of the novel (see particularly V.1, 265, and V.4, 272).

Due to both the achronological nature of *La colmena* and the extensive cast of characters, it is extremely difficult to see the chain of events in their natural order. The reader, given the time of the individual chapters and the page references in the *Censo de Personajes*, can establish the itinerary of any character for the two days. There is a complex system of chronologic relationships and of relationships between individuals that does not need to be examined in detail in order to appreciate the novel — no more than we need fully comprehend the exact nature of the relationships existing between events and individuals in the life around us in order to go on living. Cela's ideal is not the Jamesian ideal of demonstrating the arrival of the individual at an ultimate awareness of his relation to society. The Spaniard's work is a novel in much the same sense as more traditional works in its dependence on the revealing situation and the web of social circumstance. However, for Cela — and hence for the reader as well — it is essential only that life be observed and recorded while it is in motion.

As many critics have pointed out, the principal backdrop for the novel is doña Rosa's café. Cela's art is evident in the manner in which he skillfully presents in Chapter I the various customers behaving in their normal, accustomed way.[6] Despite Torrente Ballester's comment — typical of a common enough critical belief — that *La colmena* is "como un gran friso en que las amontonadas figuras se repitiesen periódicamente en actitudes distintas. No hay entre ellas jerarquía. No existe, por tanto, composición arquitectónica, sino montaje, exactamente el mismo usado por John Dos Passos en *Manhattan Transfer*",[7] there is a unity of sorts within the various sections of the novel. Chapters I and III are unified by the backdrop of the café and its clientele; Chapters II, VI, and the *Final* follow the activities of Martín Marco; Chapter V focuses on Roque's family; and Chapter IV, the center of the novel, is a series of night scenes unified by the presence of the guard Julio García Morrazo and the *sereno* Gumersindo. None of the chapters, however, has a unity of place nor a unity of action.

La colmena makes use of two distinct types of narrative units: those that are linked to each other to develop a story line and those that, although they may mention familiar persons, are essentially complete in and of themselves. Despite this evident dichotomy, each individual narrative unit has equal weight. Thus, Cela is able to advance a narrative (Martín Marco's activities, don Roque's problems, Victorita's worries) and at the same time is successful in giving the impression of a broad and populous panorama. Both are essential to produce the effect of a city in motion, where we see both the background (isolated events and individuals) and the foreground (connected events and interacting personalities).

As the novel progresses, moving from one situation to another, we are reminded of the multiplicity of people and events as well as of the effect of meeting them in their natural habitat, characteristic of *Nuevas andanzas y desventuras de Lazarillo de Tormes*. In Cela's previous novel, the events are seen through the intermediary device of a central character who is intimately involved with what he is reporting, but who, for reasons of both immaturity and proximity, is unable to render a thorough report. Most of what Lázaro reports falls within the range of the Spanish word *gracioso*. Although there are traces of bitterness and disillusion, the total effect of the novel is more entertaining than it is revealing. In *La colmena*, by doing away with a center of intelligence within the narrative, Cela has achieved a distance that renders his novel less charming but all the more clinical and penetrating.

It is this overview and this zeroing in on the subject matter that have been called Cela's camera or cinematographic technique. According to Flasher:

> The novel is a multiplicity of snapshots or sketches that follow in quick succession. To obtain them Cela uses a camera with three lenses: close-up, wide-range, and telescopic. Within the field of finder he perceives a small teeming universe with unusual intensity and accuracy of observation. His snapshots are a device that enables such a degree of concentration on each individual character and incident that there is barely any feeling of suspense.[8]

Like any analogy, the camera analogy is of value in the initial stages of examination. It conveniently establishes a point of departure by bringing together the unusual presentation of the novel and a common phenomenon of everyday life. But beyond the initial comprehension of what the author is trying to do, the analogy serves more to obscure the technique than it does to clarify it. An extension of the analogy to cover the full implications of Cela's method of reporting would pass into the absurd, once we remembered that, among other things, a camera observes only in two dimensions and does not record sound, much less achieve the feat of capturing interior monologue. Cela's perspective goes much beyond that of the camera in what it is able to record. It is, in effect, all-inclusive, omniscient, and omnipresent. The author's approach is primarily interested in *seeing*, and *La colmena* is a novel that is based upon the rewards of voyeurism.

To consider *La colmena* a novel of moral and ethical judgments is also a misleadingly simple approach. In *Nuevas andanzas y desventuras de Lazarillo de Tormes*, Lázaro was called upon to make value judgments of what he saw and what he experienced precisely because he was a part of what he was reporting. In the work under consideration, the point of reference for the novel and the events that it records are beyond the limits of the world the author has established. In this way, he is not called upon—although he could be—to evaluate what he observes. Cela has, in short, created enough distance to enable himself to remain uninvolved with his narrative on the level of the narrative; that is, neither Cela nor the reader is a member of the world under observation.[9] For Cela, history and what brings the novel and history together, can only be the cold, clinical, and uncommitted reporting of life. Cela writes in the Prologue to the third edition of his novel:

> Quisiera desarrollar la idea de que el hombre sano no tiene ideas. A veces pienso que las ideas religiosas, morales, sociales, políticas, no son sino manifestaciones de un desequilibrio del sistema nervioso. Está todavía lejano el tiempo en que se sepa que el apóstol y el iluminado son carne de manicomio, insomne y temblorosa flor de debili-

> dad. La historia, la indefectible historia, va a contrapelo de las ideas. O al margen de ellas. Para hacer historia se precisa no tener ideas, como para hacer dinero es necesario no tener escrúpulos. Las ideas y los escrúpulos – para el hombre acosado: aquel que llega a sonreír con el amargo rictus del triunfador – son una rémora. La historia es como la circulación de la sangre o como la digestión de los alimentos. Las arterias y el estómago, por donde corre y en el que se cuece la substancia histórica, son de duro y frío pedernal.[10]

There is a distinction here, of course, between the object of observations and the observer. However, given the concept that history runs contrary to ideas, it is unlikely that ideas are necessary in order to record history. The result in any case is the same: the author dispenses with moral and ethical codes in order to gain as extensive an examination as possible of mankind in motion, in the same way that mankind dispenses with morals and ethics in the normal course of routine living. The author matches wits, so to speak, with his subject matter.

The amorality of *La colmena* with regard to what it reports is a significant characteristic of the novel, but it does not imply that Cela does not sympathize deeply with the plight of his characters. He recognizes the pathos and tragedy of their situations. However, he reserves such human compassion and recognition for his Prologues, allowing the reader to draw his own conclusions from the novel. Once the critic appreciates the extent to which Cela wishes to take the pulse of life and to chart its vital functions, and once the critic understands the clinical objectivity the author wishes to simulate, then only can he accept the nature of the events portrayed in *La colmena* and the neutrality with which the author records them.

THE POSITION OF THE AUTHOR

Despite the distance from which Cela is reporting life in his novel, it does not necessarily follow that the novel represents a verbatim record of life. The author in several instances has obviously found it necessary to disturb the objectivity of his history for purposes of editing and of more convenient presentation. The author refers to himself three times in the course of the novel. Apropos of something he is relating in the second narrative unit, the author remarks: "A mí no me parece . . ." (I.2, 22). By going on to say what does not seem to him, the author creates the illusion of reporting facts and opinions as they are and not as he would believe them to be. Two other phrases remind the reader that there is indeed the *yo* of the writer (IV.41, 261) and the *vosotros* of the audience (V.2, 268). These three instances may seem insignificant, but the fact remains that elsewhere the author as Camilo José Cela has consistently attempted to remain outside the world of the narrative.

It is difficult to say whether the three examples cited are slips or are intentional interpolations. It may seem strange that one can find anything noteworthy in the problem of the presence of the author in his own work. We cannot appreciate the striving for objectivity that has characterized the modern novel until we recall that the history of the novel is a tradition of the story—something "new"—that the storyteller passes on. The author has, until quite recently, felt free to identify himself and to call upon the sympathies and imagination of his readers at crucial points in his narrative. Whether this is the best way to achieve objectivity and whether objectivity is, in effect, achieved, are moot questions at this point. In turn, the distance between reader and content is more intense when the author attempts to destroy the conventional illusion of distance. In later novels, Cela will deliberately blur the lines between what is observed and the observer, notably in *Tobogán de hambrientos*, while at the same time remaining aloof and distant. It is a precarious illusion, not fully mastered in *La colmena*.

Along with the intrusions of Cela as the author, there are the editorial notes. Which are the work of Editorial Noguer and which are the inspiration of Cela is difficult to say. One of the most important concerns the *Censo de Personajes*. In the body of the Prologue to the first edition, Cela recognizes 160 characters. A footnote reads: "N. del E. — se trata de un cálculo muy modesto por parte del autor; en el censo que figura en el presente volumen, José Manuel Caballero Bonald recuenta doscientos noventa y seis personajes imaginarios y cincuenta personajes reales: en total, trescientos cuarenta y seis" (p. 12). It would probably not be difficult to verify the existence of José Manuel Caballero Bonald. However, the reader of a novel usually does not engage in external investigations of this sort that, one way or the other, would add little or nothing to his appreciation and understanding of the novel, and the question of whether "E." equals Camilo José Cela remains.

The reader's suspicion is supported by the next *N. del E.*, which must have been the work of the author. After entering a certain letter as evidence in a sketch, a footnote explains: "La carta de Agustín Rodríguez Silva tenía puntos, pero no tenía comas; al copiarla aquí se le pusieron algunas. También se corrigieron ciertas pequeñas faltas de ortografía. (N. del E.)" (III.23, 195). This intervention on the part of the author supports our awareness of his presence and of his dominion over the material. It also raises the issue of the narrative as novel — that is, as literary contrivance — which has not been raised since *Pabellón de reposo*. In addition, there is the newly added series of footnotes in the fourth Spanish edition. They all refer to the following: "N. del A. — Mi traductora al alemán, Gerda Theile-Bruhns [[11]], me hizo ver que Padilla no es el limpia, sino el cerillero; tiene razón y rectifico el lapsus, que volvía a repetirse ocho o diez páginas más adelante. Al limpia lo bautizo — Segundo Segura — a partir de la 4.ª edición española" (I.33, 62). The fact that it is *N. del A.* is, of course, due to the nature of the intervention and is of little consequence. However, it is of consequence that Cela feels able to revise history in order to rectify a slip that only an extremely careful reader would notice. Making the change in no way clarifies the novel or even a portion of it. It serves merely as a reminder that, in the long run, despite the emotional distance between the author and his narrative, the author is still the master and creator of that material. The novel remains a contrivance he is able to change at will.

But there is another more extensive and more subtle way in which the author maintains his constant presence as the *deus ex machina* of his novel. *La colmena* is basically a novel of the present.[12] Its format is eminently oriented toward recording what is in the process of happening. But on more than twenty occasions Cela finds it necessary to refer to the past. Not that he simply describes something as having occurred yesterday, or last week, or last year. There are numerous references of this sort to the past. More significant are those instances when Cela suddenly and without warning converts his novel for the moment into a biographical sketch of a particularly interesting, although not necessarily important, figure of the narrative. Aside from the illuminating and often humorous sidelight on certain individuals provided by such a flashback, the device reveals another aspect of Cela's novelistic assumptions that further belies the camera-technique label applied by many critics. The author's point of view is not a fixed and stationary place in time or space past which the three hundred characters file in orderly but vital procession. Even in a given locale, such as the café, there is no one vantage point. We cannot imagine the author lounging at the bar or slouched at the back table as he observes the activity around him. Cela's vantage point is far above his subject matter. He is outside, but his vision is unobstructed as he looks in. Therefore, the reader cannot be surprised when the action of the novel freezes at a particular point and he is suddenly taken back in time and place as the author gives a thumbnail history of someone.

There is a constant tension in *La colmena* between dialogue and description. While it is easy enough to separate the two, it is often difficult to justify the use of one in preference to the other. Dialogue plays an important part in the novel and carries the burden of the various character portrayals. It is distinctly suited to depicting social interaction in progress. On the other hand, description is just as predominant, but is better suited to the author's desire to reveal the human personality via commentary on his behavior.[13] An individual is pinpointed and observed through dialogue. When the author shifts to commentary, the reader learns to anticipate a comment from Cela pertinent to that individual's behavior. It is a comment made possible by the distance and detachment that the author has established for himself. Whether through the use of a rapid historical or biographical flashback that belies the character's pretensions or through the effective juxtaposition of a contradictory circumstance, Cela is a master of the concise technique.

A very different matter concerns the problem of multiple reportings of the same incident. If the novel is to use as a point of departure the assumption that it creates an illusion of reality, a reality that the reader is permitted to observe only by a stroke of good fortune, it follows that the novel must be irreproachable in terms of verisimilitude. However, since Cela appears not to be writing on the assumption that his novel is an illusion of reality, he allows himself certain liberties within the realm of what is plausible in the interest of probing his material more deeply. One such liberty is the freedom to report the same incident twice or, better, to record the same dialogue twice, both times differently. Cela does this several times. The variation need not be extensive. Even the minutest of changes immediately destroys the semblance of a world in which a given event can have been seen only at a given time by a given individual (the author) in a single given way. For example, when Pepe the waiter returns after having thrown Martín Marco out of doña Rosa's café for being unable to pay, the exchange of dialogue is as follows:

> —Ven acá.
> Pepe casi no se atreve a mirarla.
> —¿Qué quiere?
> —¿Le has arreado?
> —Sí, señorita.
> —¿Cuántas?
> —Dos.

La dueña entorna los ojitos tras los cristales, saca las manos de los bolsillos y se los pasa por la cara, donde apuntan los cañotes de la barba, mal tapados por los polvos de arroz.

—¿Dónde se las has dado?

—Donde pude; en las piernas.

—Bien hecho. ¡Para que aprenda! Así otra vez no querrá robarle el dinero a las gentes honradas! (I.25, 53)

When the same event is reported in the following chapter, the dialogue has changed to the following:

—Oye, ven acá.

El camarero se le acercó.

—¿Le has arreado?

—Sí, señorita.

—¿Cuántas?

—Dos.

—¿Dónde?

—Donde pude, en las piernas.

—¡Bien hech! ¡Por mangante! (II.3, 86–87)

Such a procedure strikes at the roots of the novel as it is traditionally thought to be. It tends as well to refute the critical position that affirms Cela's novel is a patchwork quilt of narrative units thrown together and palmed off as a picture of society. Cela is equally interested in establishing the distance and devices for commentary that have been discussed. Although Cela does not make a moral judgment on what he presents, his own position with reference to the work permits him the neutral commentary that gives the novel its depth of perception.

CHARACTERIZATION

Individuals are the the basis of *La colmena.* If there were no other evidence available, the presence alone of the *Censo de Personajes*, with its page references and character sketches, would be ample testimony to the important role played by people in the work. *La colmena* is one continuous interplay of people. Although the chronology is fragmented, the novel is able to develop a world based upon the activities of individuals in time.

Cela's work strives for a simultaneity of time and place, and the devices chosen to effect this merger on the abstract level limit the extent to which he can employ plot; thus, the action is limited to a two-day span for the main body of the novel. Rejecting extended plot development as a means of character portrayal, Cela uses the two methods of presentation mentioned previously: biographical sketch and juxtaposition for contrast. It would be impossible to document all of the ways in which these two techniques are used. Perhaps two examples will suffice.

The first example demonstrates the use of juxtaposition for purposes of contrast. Doña Rosa is advising Elvira, a neighborhood prostitute, to take up with don Pablo. Elvira replies:

> —[. . .]Es un tío muy exigente. Y además un baboso. Al final yo le aborrecía, ¡qué quiere usted!, ya me daba hasta repugnancia.
>
> Doña Rosa pone la dulce voz, la persuasiva voz de los consejos.
>
> —¡Hay que tener más paciencia, Elvirita! ¡Usted es aún muy niña!
>
> —¿Usted cree?
>
> La señorita Elvirita escupe debajo de la mesa y se seca la boca con la vuelta de un guante. (I.12, 35)

The second example demonstrates how Cela employs background information as well as juxtaposition to advantage in delineating a character's personality:

> Doña Juana, con la vista clavada en el suelo, reanudó su tema: el asesinato de doña Margot.
>
> —¡Con una toalla! ¿Usted cree que hay derecho? ¡Con una toalla! ¡Qué falta de consideración para una ancianita! El criminal la ahorcó con una toalla como si fuera un pollo. En la mano le puso una flor. La pobre se quedó con los ojos abiertos, según dicen parecía una lechuza, yo no tuve valor para verla; a mí estas cosas me impresionan mucho. Yo no quisiera equivocarme, pero a mí me da el olfato que su niño debe andar mezclado en todo esto. El hijo de

doña Margot, que en paz descanse, era mariquita, ¿sabe usted?, andaba en muy malas compañías. Mi pobre marido siempre lo decía: quien mal anda, mal acaba.

El difunto marido de doña Juana, don Gonzalo Sisemón, había acabado sus días en un prostíbulo de tercera clase, una tarde que le falló el corazón. Sus amigos lo tuvieron que traer en un taxi, por la noche, para evitar complicaciones. A doña Juana le dijeron que se había muerto en la cola de Jesús de Medinaceli, y doña Juana se lo creyó. El cadáver de don Gonzalo venía sin tirantes, pero doña Juana no cayó en el detalle. [[14]]

—¡Pobre Gonzalo! —decía, ¡pobre Gonzalo! ¡Lo único que me reconforta es pensar que se ha ido derechito al cielo, que a estas horas estará mucho mejor que nosotros! ¡Pobre Gonzalo!

Doña Asunción, como quien oye llover, sigue con lo de la Paquita. (V.5, 278–79)

La colmena is constructed upon the procedure demonstrated in the foregoing passages. Once the reader has accepted the *de facto* novelistic assumption proposed by Cela and the constant tension and interplay between the characters' dialogues and the author's commentaries upon them, he may achieve a rather complete understanding of the motives of the personalities in *La colmena.*

Since Martín Marco is one of the most important characters in the novel, if not the principal one, an examination of some of the ways in which he is presented will help to clarify Cela's techniques of characterization.[15]

In Chapter I, Martín appears only once, when he is tossed out of doña Rosa's café. Although he is not identified, Cela reveals some of his background in a biographical sketch. Martín appears again in Chapter II, where he is the unifying force. He appears nine times periodically throughout the first two thirds of the chapter, and the continuity of his actions punctuates the various evening scenes. The author extends Martín's biography and plays him against several people, notably his charitable sister and his hardhearted brother-in-law. In Chapter II, doña Margot's body is found, and if Marco is to be suspected of her murder, Cela's technique is a negative one, for her body is found in the latter third of the chapter in which Martín does not appear.

Martín appears three times in Chapter III, when he is seen in the company of several former classmates, thus revealing a level of his personality different from the one that emerges in the company of present friends and relatives. Chapter IV is a series of late-evening street scenes in which Martín figures prominently. The chapter ends with his falling asleep in the arms of a prostitute in a house whose madam has a maternal affection for him. The result is yet a third level of Martín's personality.

Chapter V includes Martín only twice, both times in the same situation. Martín has acquired some money and returns to doña Rosa's café. As a paying customer he is able to laugh in the face of the proprietress who the previous day had ordered his expulsion. Chapter VI is the morning following Chapter IV. Still in the brothel, Martín is played against his companion of the previous night in a series of dialogue exchanges.

However, it is in the *Final* that Cela uses the technique of juxtaposition to greatest advantage. Where previously he had contrasted situations and circumstances within the narrative units, here he contrasts Marco and several others from one narrative unit to another. By alternating sketches of Marco, who is ignorant of what is about to befall him, with sketches describing his acquaintances' awareness of the situation, Cela is able to end his novel with a final statement on the irony of Martín Marco's aimless life as well as with a broad implication as to the irony of life in general. Since Martín Marco serves as a pivotal point of reference to which the narrative constantly returns, the essential aimlessness of his existence stands out vividly. The structure of *La colmena* is designed to emphasize this aimlessness. Nevertheless, Martín's plight is a condition shared by the community of *La colmena* as a whole. Indeed, a good portion of the interest of the novel stems from the ever-changing direction of its characters' lives. The element of surprise is ever present, and the various threads of narrative maintain the initial impression of life as a gigantic *non sequitur.* This impression is fostered by the fragmentary nature of the make-up of the novel and by the lack of a significant pattern of events, assuming that the reader is able to recall exactly what does happen to any one character out of the three hundred. Martín is a novelistic expedient forced by the structure of *La colmena.* When compared with the other characters of the novel, nothing marks him as outstanding. He is one among many who are alike in their problems and sufferings. His activities are placed in relief solely for the purposes of establishing a point of reference for the narrative and to provide a vertebra for a novel which to many critics seems to be the invertebrate novel without equal. On the basis of Martín's life, as it is established by the novel's structure, and on the basis of its relevancy to life in general, any thematic analysis of *La colmena* would have to consider Marco as an important point of departure.

Cela is unwilling to ensconce himself behind the structure of *La colmena* as he did in *La familia de Pascual Duarte*. He no longer finds it expedient to create the illusion of the characters' unfolding their personalities before us through their behavior in revealing situations. In a word, he shuns the Jamesian ideal of the novel. Cela's novel seeks and finds new ways of portraying human behavior, ways that involve the author's arranging reality in order that the reader may most conveniently understand whatever it is that the novelist would have him understand. Many commentators have asked rhetorically, apropos of the vision of the novel, "But isn't there more to life than just this?" Perhaps there is. The fact remains that no novel describes *all* of the possibilities of life. Furthermore, if we once accept the possibility of life being as Cela describes it in the sector of Madrid society he chooses to portray, it is difficult for us to reject the aspects of life Cela does present.

La colmena goes beyond being merely a sociological casebook. Cela enjoys a unique position with regard to the content of the work. Although his program for the novel calls for taking the pulse of life, it brings with it a superior status for the author, a status the reader shares. We witness life with the author and with him are prevented from becoming involved in it. Cela, indeed, specifically warns, although with the bitterest of ironies, "No merece la pena que nos dejemos invadir por la tristeza. La tristeza también es un atavismo" (p. 16). In this distance and in this detachment, as well as in the ensuing control the author has over his novelistic material, Cela's program differs markedly from the similar "take-the-pulse-of-life" programs of realism and naturalism.

La colmena represents a particularly important point in Cela's career because it is the first of his novels to put into effect a well-defined and original program for the novel. *La familia de Pascual Duarte* and *Nuevas andanzas y desventuras de Lazarillo de Tormes*, while demonstrating the author's potential as an innovator, are essentially traditional novels. *Pabellón de reposo* is a frank experiment with the novel, which, lacking a definite program, remains interesting but not particularly significant. With *La colmena*, Cela seems to have found his true vein in the novel. Although the following chapters discuss other modes of the novel in Cela's fiction, it is necessary to keep in mind Cela's proposal as articulated by this novel. In considering Cela's more recent works, it will become evident that he has returned to the inspiration that produced *La colmena*.

5

Mrs. Caldwell habla con su hijo:

AN EXPERIMENT IN THE NEW NOVEL

THE NOVEL that followed *La colmena* in mid-1953 was the radically different *Mrs. Caldwell habla con su hijo.*[1] Cela continued to adhere in his fifth novel to his fundamental principle that the novel is basically a documentary form providing information concerning the human animal. However, any similarity to *La colmena* is obscured by Cela's experimentation with the "new novel." In the course of this chapter, the background and premises of the term "new novel" will be discussed, and *Mrs. Caldwell* will be analyzed as a possible manifestation of that genre in Spain.

Plot

Cela, as he explains in a brief introductory note, met Mrs. Caldwell in Pastrana during the wanderings that resulted in his *Viaje a la Alcarria.*[2] The book he presents to the public consists of a set of letters written by Mrs. Caldwell to her dead son Eliacim, who was lost at sea with H.M.S. *Furious.* Cela has been willed the papers by Mrs. Caldwell, who dies in the Royal Insane Asylum in London. The 212 letters reveal Mrs. Caldwell's mental deterioration and detail her transfer to the asylum. It soon becomes apparent why Mrs. Caldwell writes to her dead son instead of keeping a more conventional diary. Her son dead, Mrs. Caldwell betrays her tenacious and incestuous love for him without fear of shame. Since this theme of the novel has been adequately dealt with elsewhere, it is not necessary to stress the particulars here.[3] The reader with an experienced imagination and a rudimentary acquaintance with popular Freudianism can easily grasp Cela's intent.[4]

The portrayal of Mrs. Caldwell's sexual deviation as it emerges through her interests and self-confessed fetishes constitutes the novel's plot. Although there are many random observations that are not easily related to this theme, it is the only unifying motif of the novel.[5]

Formal and Structural Considerations

THE NEW NOVEL IN FRANCE

In the mid-fifties a form of the novel emerged in France associated with names of writers like Samuel Beckett, Michel Butor, Alain Robbe-Grillet, and Nathalie Sarraute, to name a few who have gained a wide audience through translation of their work. The *nouveau roman*, or "new novel," has had an impact upon literature sufficient to be considered a separate and distinct mode of fiction.[6] A revolt against the traditional Balzacian or Jamesian novel, with its assumption that the personality of an individual is an isolable and definable constant, the new novel may also be considered a revolt against the existential ethic in the novel, which has often emphasized, if not the adherence to a particular moral and ethical standard, the involvement of the author in a very personal way with his subject matter. Indeed, out of this double revolt have come the two most salient characteristics of the new novel: a belief in the absolute relativity and mutability of the universe, including human behavior, and a conviction of the necessity for a clinical detachment in reporting this "continuum of existence," if we may coin a term that reflects the arbitrary nature of the particular activity observed.[7]

Once the integrity of the individual personality has been denied, a substitute must be sought for exposition by the author. While it would be absurd to deny that the author of a novel is omniscient or omnipresent in relation to his novel, the problem concerns how he is to effect the position of being merely a casual observer or, better, of not being present at all. This question has frequently been solved by substituting analysis, in which the author comments, with the point-of-view technique. Actions are carried out and dialogues are engaged in at given points in space and at given moments in time that chance to coincide with the instance of the novel. The result is a continual feeling of eavesdropping on the part of the reader.[8]

It would naturally follow that the themes, heroes, and structural devices of the new novel are at variance with the older tradition and in agreement with the limitations imposed by this new concept of the novel. Most notable is a concentration upon things: things in relation to events and things in relation to individuals. This is part of the behavioristic, nonmoral, nonethical approach to characters and incidents. The author must rely upon what is seen and what is expressed. He no longer believes that he can determine their why and wherefore, and he no longer believes that the individual himself, formerly the rational man, can. As Le Sage observes with regard to Robbe-Grillet:

> Not only has he filled his novels with minute descriptions of objects devoid of intrinsic human values and qualities, but, in his essays, by damning and derisive phrases like "subject interiority" and "the romantic heart of things" (borrowed from Barthes), he has struck repeatedly at subjectivism. All the new novelists, however, follow this method and the objective that Husserl formulated when he proposed returning to things. The method is completely neutral, postulating no realistic or idealistic metaphysic—nothing, as Robbe-Grillet says, that would imply essentialism or pre-established order. It amounts merely to a description of the world such as it appears to a completely naive consciousness. The writer's purpose is the same as the philosopher's: to depict the world as it is illuminated by consciousness and to depict consciousness itself in its act of perceiving and giving sense to the world.[9]

A second characteristic result of the initial assumptions of the new novel is the distortion and fragmentation of chronology. Interested in the effects to be gained by distorting the natural chronology of events in *Pabellón de reposo* and *La colmena*, Cela replaces astronomical time with a readily observable pattern that stands in lieu of the natural sequence of events. It has been suggested that this is a device employed to create the illusion of simultaneity and to give the feeling that an arbitrarily chosen period of time is final and closed. The new novel employs much the same technique. Since it rejects a priori assumptions and values with regard to the material treated, any point along the continuum of events in the universe is equally valid and no more important or interesting than any other. The result is a complete arbitrariness as far as the two outer limits (beginning and end) of the novel are concerned. The same is true of *Pabellón de reposo* and *La colmena*. But once the arbitrary period had been chosen, an attempt was made to make the final boundary seem significant: in *Pabellón*, the deaths of the patients; in *La colmena*, the mystery of Martín Marco.

Once the arbitrary boundaries have delimited the novel by clock time, the author proceeds to allow subjective time to dominate his work. In place of sequences of cause-and-effect events, developed along a line of durational time, the reader finds instead artificial and contrived formal patternings not unlike those found in *Pabellón de reposo*. Le Sage summarizes the intent of this chronological fragmentation and subsequent formal schematization as follows:

> But differing from Faulkner and from the English stream-of-consciousness writers, from whom these narrative devices were borrowed, the new French writers have, at least more patently, a philosophical objective in mind. Formal patterns are for them actually more than the means of endowing their works with esthetic significance or even of depicting the process of the psyche and the human adventure on earth. By using formal patterns to present life in the novel, the new writers further an ulterior purpose dear

to their hearts – that of undermining the notions of chronology, of casuality, and all the other props of the common-sense universe.[10]

These, then, are the major characteristics of the French new novel.[11] One further theoretical problem remains to be dealt with before proceeding to an examination of *Mrs. Caldwell.* That problem concerns the relationship of the French new novel to the concept of the novel as we have used it in discussing *La colmena* and to psychological introspection as we have applied it to *Pabellón de reposo.*

It would seem clear that the new novel does not fit into the pattern of the novel as a socially oriented mode of fiction. It is fiction in a different sense of the word and a novel only in the sense that any extended prose fiction narrative is called a novel. The French new novel is inherently different from the fictional mode to which I have assigned *Pascual Duarte, Lazarillo de Tormes,* and *La colmena.*

It may be argued that the new novel, as does the novel of psychological introspection, concentrates its attention upon the circumstances in relation to the individual rather than upon the individual in relation to the circumstances. Yet, both of the more traditional forms of the novel assume the possibility of revealing and isolating the traits of an individual's personality. The difference is to be found in the approaches employed. A novel of psychological introspection is concerned with elucidating the emotions of the characters through their own self-examination. The experiences they undergo are designed to reveal the profoundest aspects of their soul. In both the Jamesian novel and the introspective novel, the individual remains recognizable and identifiable. Although his personality may not remain stable, the reader is able to say wherein it has fluctuated or undergone a change. *Pabellón de reposo* is introspective as a result of the unusual and exaggerated circumstances of the seven individuals presented. Their hospitalization and the sure promise of death are circumstances designed to elicit emotions that would probably not be forthcoming in the day-to-day routine of life outside the walls of the sanitarium. The new novel has none of these characteristics. Its rejection of the possibility of revealing a character's personality and the attempt to be casual about the events and circumstances chosen for portrayal are significant exceptions to practice in the novel of psychological introspection. For these reasons, *Pabellón de reposo* and *Mrs. Caldwell* are dealt with separately as two different modes of narrative prose fiction.

FORMAL ELEMENTS

Mrs. Caldwell contains 212 chapters. Chapters 14 and 60 are represented by two versions. The first 208 chapters are written elsewhere; the last four are *Cartas desde el Real Hospital de Lunáticos*. There is no symmetry created by the various narrative units, and it would be useless to assign the separate chapters to types of content, because they lack structural significance. This lack of symmetry is a marked difference between *Mrs. Caldwell* and *Pabellón de reposo*, which has a structural pattern in the mere arrangement of the narrative. The impression is that the 212 chapters were assembled at random, and, indeed, any justification for their present order would be forced to rely upon a nonexistent internal development of Mrs. Caldwell's affliction.

Topics covered by Mrs. Caldwell in her writings, which are in the nature of a diary, fall into the following broad categories: herself, her son, her family, her acquaintances, strangers, and things. It is evident that the categories are insignificant, since they include virtually everything that a woman of Mrs. Caldwell's middle-class standing would be likely to find noteworthy. Abstract subjects are lacking as topics for discussion, and any occasion for philosophizing is suggested by things. Random objects as well as the personal effects of both Mrs. Caldwell and her son serve to conjure up memories and observations, and the titles of many of the chapters point to the preponderant interest in tangible objects. Still, no pattern emerges. Although Cela has responded to one of the technical criteria of the new novel, the destruction of chronology, he has not substituted the corresponding technical innovation of patterning.

PERSPECTIVE AND POINT OF VIEW

In *Mrs. Caldwell* neither Cela nor his representative appears. With the exception of the opening *Advertencia* and the closing *Otra advertencia,* it is Mrs. Caldwell alone who speaks. The only breaks in the reader's contact with her diary come in the two footnotes signed "N. del T.," in which Cela remarks, on two occasions, on the illegibility of the manuscript. The result is to maintain the fiction that Mrs. Caldwell is an externally identifiable person and an acquaintance of the author. The desire is to give a validity outside the novel to writings that, because of their nature and the manner in which they are presented, could easily be rejected as absurd and unlikely.

Mrs. Caldwell is similar in this respect to *La familia de Pascual Duarte* and *Nuevas andanzas y desventuras de Lazarillo de Tormes.* All three novels attempt to establish an external point of reference in order to lend a nonfictional verisimilitude to their contents. Although it is realized differently, such a desire is also present in *Pabellón de reposo* and in *La colmena.* In all five works Cela's constant concern is that his readers come to the conclusion that he is presenting them, not with fiction, but with human documentation. (We assume that Cela is speaking ironically when he says that *Pabellón de reposo* is only fiction and therefore it does not impinge upon the "reality" of the reader.) While it is true that a novel cannot dispense entirely with artifice and contrivance, the author uses these devices in order to create the illusion that artifice and contrivance are not present in the work. That some critics are unable to accept such a procedure explains in part the unfavorable treatment they have accorded Cela's novels.

It remains to be seen whether the novel can dispense with the aura of fiction and microcosmic completeness that we associate with it, or whether our casual and critical tastes can be re-educated by the concerted attempts of the new novelists, including Cela. Certainly, the discussion and understanding of the basis of these attempts can do much in the way of assuring mature and fair evaluations.

Many of the problems concerning the validity of the presentation of events in *La familia de Pascual Duarte* arise also in *Mrs. Caldwell.* Because of the woman's derangement, the reader assigns very little reliability to her observations, especially those regarding her deceased husband and her drowned son Eliacim. Although the reader is able to draw some conclusions concerning both Mr. Caldwell and Eliacim from what Mrs. Caldwell writes, the structure of the novel and the feelings of the woman toward the two dissuade the reader from trusting her portrayals. Mr. Caldwell emerges as an inept and bungling husband, a man held in contempt by his wife; her candid confessions inform us that he was a cuckold. This in itself would give the reader sufficient reason to appreciate Mrs. Caldwell's sentiments. The perceptive reader's initial suspicions concerning the woman's sentiments toward her son are soon confirmed, and her incestuous love for Eliacim explains even better than her own statements Mrs. Caldwell's disdain for her husband. To the degree to which it exists, this irony enjoyed by the reader against Mrs. Caldwell provides an internal device by which he can measure the sincerity and the validity of Mrs. Caldwell's statements.

Since the reader has no other knowledge about Eliacim, it is difficult to evaluate the portrait of him that emerges from the diary. The son seems to have been somewhat of a mama's boy and a prig. A mother's feeling of possessiveness toward her only son is natural, and Mrs. Caldwell's exaggerated attachment provides a very simple explanation for his apparent overdependence. The mother discusses, in addition to the mother-son relationship, Eliacim's relations with other people and his career.

What the reader suspects most strongly is that Mrs. Caldwell projects her various states of mind upon the things and persons around her. In turn, she sees in these things and persons a suggestion of her own thoughts. The chapters of the diary represent the categorization of her thoughts on the basis of external *realia.* There is reason to believe that Mrs. Caldwell sees in her son not only an Eliacim as she would want him to be, but also an Eliacim who suffers from her own *idées fixes.* The result is a passage like the following, in which Mrs. Caldwell attributes to Eliacim her own preoccupation with fetishes:

> CAP.146. LOS FETICHES
>
> Tú, Eliacim, siempre habías sido muy aficionado a los fetiches. Sobre todos los fetiches, Eliacim, tú preferías los de hueso, los de plata, los de madera y los de hierro, por este orden; los de cobre los despreciabas y los de pasta no podías ni verlos. En esto, como en todo, hay preferencias y simpatías y aborrecimientos y antipatías. Es cosa en la que no entro.[. . .]
>
> Tú siempre fuiste muy aficionado a los fetiches, hijo mío, y tu afición, con tu colección, la heredé yo.
>
> A veces, cuando no tengo nada que hacer, limpio, uno por uno, tus fetiches; me gusta conservarlos bien. (pp. 145–46)

Mrs. Caldwell's interest in fetishes is apparent throughout the novel and is symptomatic of her illness. Many of the things she collects, preserves, and remarks upon are either overt sexual symbols or articles obviously suggestive of her son. They are fetishes in the psychiatric sense of the word, evoking sexual relationships. Such a predominant interest in *realia* is characteristic of the new novel and demonstrates the link between the devices of Cela's novel and the possible external manifestations of the derangement that it describes. The result is that the novel has no point of reference which has any reliability for the reader. The various things have no value in themselves, and the events and people described by the narrator seem to be at a great distance, as if they had never existed. The reader is forced to think continually in abstract terms. In order to derive any adequate meaning from the novel, it is necessary to view what is presented in clinical terms. Whether a particular point raised in the novel contributes or detracts from our amateur psychiatric analysis of Mrs. Caldwell becomes singularly important. The reader does not follow the woman's writings in order to see a narrative unfolding but to gain raw material to be used in his analysis of the narrator. Cela's novel emerges as a purported source of information concerning the human psyche rather than a unified and coherent portrayal of it in terms of its own circumstance.

Nevertheless, the reader finds it difficult to determine when Mrs. Caldwell is being candid and when she is simulating sincerity and frankness. A similar problem arises in connection with Pascual Duarte, but only an inborn cynicism toward all confessions could put in doubt Duarte's sober admissions and exculpations. With Mrs. Caldwell, doubt is increased because of her revealed mental deterioration. Paul Ilie seems to summarize Cela's intent when he speaks of demonstrating "el método que el autor emplea de destruir las tradicionales dimensiones estructurales en su esfuerzo por crear una nueva novela psicológica."[12] The question remains as to whether the novel constitutes a sufficient source of information for the personality and character of Mrs. Caldwell. Certainly the structural perspective prevents the reader from learning all he would like to know.

The extremely fragmentary nature of *Mrs. Caldwell* is essential to the approach to the description of reality found in the new novel. It is an approach intimately linked to the desire to shun the psychological portrayal of an individual, whether in terms of his external circumstance or in terms of his inner conflicts. Perhaps this is why Cela has chosen to present *Mrs. Caldwell* from one person's point of view. If such is the case, it is a successful way of frustrating the reader's attempt to psychoanalyze Mrs. Caldwell.

This approach, however, is not merely a result of the author's whim to prevent the reader from understanding Mrs. Caldwell fully. To attribute such a procedure to whim, as some critics have done, is to doubt Cela's integrity as an artist.

Reconsidering the basic premise of the new novel that two individuals can never presume to understand each other completely, one can understand why the author, representing the point of view of one individual, refuses to pretend to be able to plumb the depths of another person's mind. The problem is compounded by the fact that the audience, in turn, constitutes an infinite extension of the basic incapacity for human understanding with a multiple range of possible misunderstandings. The solution of the new novelist is to present a "selection," a random sampling of casual states of mind. Conclusions, right or wrong, are to be drawn exclusively from such a random sampling.

Mrs. Caldwell has been called a psychological novel, but it is evident that it does not meet the popular concept of a psychological novel. Nathalie Sarraute writes of how the novel has freed itself from individual psychology and turned its attention to those outward, separate, and unique manifestations of his psychology:

> Or, nous l'avons vu, les personnages, tels que les concevait le vieux roman (et tout le vieil appareil qui servait à le mettre en valeur), ne parviennent plus à contenir la realité psychologique actuelle. Au lieu, comme autrefois, de la révéler, ils l'escamotent.
>
> Aussi, par une évolution analogue à celle de la peinture — bien qu'infiniment plus timide et plus lente, coupée de longs arrêts et de reculs — l'élément pictural, se libère insensiblement de l'objet avec lequel il faisait corps. Il tend à se suffire à lui-même et à se passer le plus possible de support. C'est sur lui que tout l'effort de recherche du romancier se concentre, et sur lui que doit porter tout l'effort d'attention du lecteur.[13]

Mrs. Caldwell would appear to be this type of psychological novel.

Achronology is a useful term in characterizing the treatment of time in *Mrs. Caldwell.* One cannot speak of either an astronomical chronology or an antichronology. Time in the durational or mathematical sense simply does not exist for the majority of the new novels. Such a phenomenon is the direct result of the desire to portray states of mind observed at random points in time. There is no need to relate the points along a time continuum; the novelist-observer cannot and will not predict what the gaps may have represented. The result is either a series of narrative tableaux that are evidently random moments, with the moments identified in time, or equally random moments that remain unidentified. Cela accepts the latter possibility in his novel. The only argument for the arrangement of the novel concerns the sheer physical and graphical necessities of the book as a published item: it has covers (a beginning and an end), and it has consecutive, attached pages (order).

It would be difficult to argue in favor of the order Cela has given the 212 chapters of the novel. Each chapter is autonomous, with the exception of the two (14 and 60) for which variants are given. The outer limits, the "beginning" and the "end" of Cela's novel, are completely arbitrary; the diary ends only because there are no more entries and because some of the extant entries are illegible. The novel does not end for any of the reasons traditionally associated with the closing pages of a narrative, such as narrative plateau, resolution of conflicts, natural end of a sequence of events. Indeed, the entrance of Mrs. Caldwell into the insane asylum at such an advanced point in the work opens up many vistas for psychological portrayal that in the end are left unexploited.

AESTHETIC DISTANCE

Mrs. Caldwell is unique among Cela's novels. Given its nature and given Cela's novels as a whole, it is surprising that the author has managed to free himself so completely from the narrative. He appears in the two *advertencias* solely for the purpose of establishing the origin of the papers that make up the book.[14] It is this complete absence of the author's commentary that constitutes the basic and fundamental difference between *Mrs. Caldwell* and its predecessor *La colmena.*

Although there are good reasons to consider the approaches of the two novels as manifestations of the same mode of fiction, their differences are greater than their similarities. It is basically true that both *La colmena* and *Mrs. Caldwell* intend to be more documentary than novelistic in nature, if one understands *documentary* to mean the presentation of isolated bits of evidence and *novelistic* to refer to the telling of a connected tale. Both works are *histories* in Cela's definition, a term that attempts to avoid the connotation of fabrication usually associated with the term *novel*. However, in *La colmena*, the history, the documented evidence presented in support of an implicit a priori vision of mankind, is discussed at the same time that it is being given. The reader has every reason to believe that the discussions and the arrangement of the content for maximum effect are the work of one commentator with one fixed and omniscient point of view. It would be natural to assume that the commentator is the author himself. Actually, the question is not whose point of view enjoys such a favorable perspective, but that such a point of view exists at all. Such a superior perspective for the author-narrator corresponds to Cela's concept of the novel as articulated in the Prologue. Both the reader and the author are aware that the novel is someone's fabrication, and it is futile to pretend that the novel portrays a real and verifiable series of events with correspondingly real people. Since both parties are aware of this fact, no end is served by maintaining the semblance of a hermetically sealed microcosm. Perhaps by directly intervening and ordering the little world of fiction, more insights concerning human behavior can be brought to light. According to Cela, the exegesis of humanity is the only purpose of the novel, and it should be served by whatever means are available.

While no one would be willing to deny the constant hand of the novelist in the fabrication of his novel, it must be realized that in *Mrs. Caldwell* there is no internal evidence that anyone but Mrs. Caldwell is responsible for her diary. That is to say, in his fifth novel Cela chooses to maintain the semblance of an autonomous fictional realm. Such a decision is not due to any belief on the part of the new novelist that this semblance should be maintained. Rather, the dispensing with the interaction between the superior author and his material is a reflection of quite a different tendency in the new novel. In *La colmena* the author is clinically detached but still finds it expedient to deal directly with his material. He observes the actions of his characters and makes them act for our benefit. Neither the reader nor the author is intended to identify with the characters of the novel. Still, there is a tension inherent in *La colmena*, and the reader is often hard put to determine where the characters leave off and Cela begins. By not dealing directly with the narrative that constitutes *Mrs. Caldwell*, any tension is done away with, and the detachment of both author and reader is permanently established. In order to ensure complete alienation, Cela has recourse to the techniques of the *Verfremdungseffekt*.

Verfremdungseffekt (Spanish *enajenación*) is a neologism created by Bertolt Brecht.[15] It essentially means, in the context of both the new novel and the new theater, the creation of an extreme distance between the spectacle and the spectator so that normal interaction is destroyed. In the dramatic modes of Pirandello the distance is reduced to the vanishing point; in the works of Brecht it is drawn out to infinity. The result in both cases is severe distortion and lack of perspective. The audience is unable to ascertain its relationship to what it is observing. Either the observer is part of the work or the work is so far removed that no rapport is ever established.

Such a distortion of the aesthetic distance is equally applicable to the modes of fiction under discussion. Although there is little possibility of identification, the distance between the reader and the characters of *La colmena* is extended. In *Mrs. Caldwell* this distance is exaggerated. Speaking of surrealism in *Mrs. Caldwell* and the problems of interpretation, Paul Ilie concludes: "La dificultad de la novela surge de tres condiciones: una mentalidad ajena a la del lector; una falta de continuidad narrativa que da por resultado contextos breves e independientes; un tipo de símbolos infradesarrollados [i.e., with private meanings]."[16] All three of these considerations and others are characteristic of the techniques for distancing which Cela utilizes.

The limitation imposed by the presentation from one person's point of view is the most elementary of the ways in which Cela alienates his reader from the subject at hand. The reader is unable to measure the narrative and the narrator's sincerity against any other points of reference and must take Mrs. Caldwell's statements at face value. Any further interpretation of them is merely unjustifiable conjecture. While *Mrs. Caldwell* is innovative in the narrational use of the second person, the fact that there is only one narrator, whose statements are never challenged, results in the same set of reader-novel relationships that would exist were the narration in the third person. Of course, Mrs. Caldwell, in the last analysis, is functioning as a third-person narrator.

Of considerably more importance is the alienating effect of Mrs. Caldwell's personality, augmented by her socially disapproved aberration. It is not so much her incestuous love for her son that alienates the reader's sympathy, for a skilled artist is able to enlist the sympathies of the audience for any human failing when he wants to. But Cela appears not to want the reader's sympathy for Mrs. Caldwell; rather, he appears to cultivate actively our distaste for her. This is accomplished through the structure of the novel and the revelation of Mrs. Caldwell's personality. The diarist reveals herself to be both mediocre in sensitivity and lacking in appeal as a person. Mrs. Caldwell's letters to her son are characterized by a tone of pouting. When one adds to her disagreeable personality the perverted affection toward Eliacim, the effect is extremely distasteful for the reader, who, one might expect, is quite conventional. In short, Mrs. Caldwell, if we are to accept Cela's pretense for the novel, is entirely responsible for the unfavorable impression she makes. She is both petty and immoral; both accusations are supported by her own words. The total effect is increased by the complete lack of any let-up in her portrayal. As long as we are reading the novel, we must adhere to the unilateral and alienating presentation by Mrs. Caldwell.

The foregoing two points would be adequate enough to create distance between the content of the novel and the charitable emotions of the reader, but Cela goes even further. As we know from Cela's introductory remarks, Mrs. Caldwell died in an insane asylum. We also know that her last four letters originate from the asylum. Thus, to the unilateral point of view and to the woman's immorality the author adds insanity as an element to alienate the reader. We can more readily accept emotional incapacity as a human failing than incest, and Mrs. Caldwell's insanity functions more in terms of purely physical distancing, much like the unilateral point of view. If Mrs. Caldwell is insane, then we have an even stronger reason to doubt her statements. In this way the reader is twice removed from the subject of her letters. This alone would be an indifferent alienation; to it we add moral indignation.

The remaining two ways in which Cela creates the feeling of total alienation on the part of the reader are fragmentation and the use of things as narrative stimuli, two devices in accord with the principles of the new novel. The tenets of the new novel encourage fragmentation of the narrative by appealing to the fact that no novel can give a total account of all of the facets of any one event. Since the reality of the novel must be fragmentary, the new novelist makes a virtue out of a necessity. He strives openly for the effect produced by disjointed pieces, a procedure that explains the achronological and alogical sequence of Mrs. Caldwell's various letters. In terms of the impact of such a technique, the fragmentary nature of the evidence derives from Cela's concerted attempt to make it difficult for the reader to approach the novel with any degree of forthrightness.

The abundant use of physical *realia* in the new novel is an inheritance from Sartre and the existentialists, who, in insisting that existence precedes essence, have placed a strong emphasis upon the physical reality of the universe. The individual is identified with the things with which he surrounds himself, things that he invests with a special meaning understood only by him. It is not too important whether the things employed in order to refer to a character and to his revealed states of mind are identified as symbols. Since physical *realia* have the meaning the user chooses to give them, they are essentially private symbols lacking the universal significance that would imply essence before existence. Thus, a given object on different occasions might have different meanings for the same person. Each object becomes a mirror that reflects the state of mind at present. Such a procedure implies a constant externalizing of the states of mind, an implication enthusiastically in accord with the tenets of the new novel. The procedure also allows a set of purely casual and random objects to become the focal points of the narrative; almost anything can be a stimulus for the narrative.

Cela in this novel, finds this procedure particularly useful. Not only does it promote alienation by continually placing inanimate objects between the reader and Mrs. Caldwell, but this technique also reveals Mrs. Caldwell's sick mind. Things pertaining to and suggestive of Eliacim come to constitute fetishes for the mother, that serve to materialize and externalize the internal and abstract feelings of the woman. The physical *realia* that Mrs. Caldwell uses do not constitute true symbols because neither their individual presence nor their symbology is consistent throughout the novel. They are momentary occurrences that give impetus and direction to the novel, supporting and furthering the alienation of the reader.

Mrs. Caldwell is essentially an original experiment for Cela. Although the work does not represent a radical departure from the author's previous fictional endeavors, it seeks to redefine certain elements of the novel and to clarify certain other techniques. Cela saw the opportunity in writing *Mrs. Caldwell* to concentrate upon an idea he articulates in a later prologue to *La colmena*, that sadness is an atavism. Mrs. Caldwell's personality provided the occasion to experiment with the belief that the novel should be a means of gaining information and insight into the human situation. In order to take the best advantage of the documentary and clinical possibilities of the novel, it is necessary that the reader not become involved, not sympathize with the characters presented. The audience is to stand back, behind the lines of the struggle, so to speak, and observe the Lilliputian world of the novel play out its grim parts. The fact that the reader would want to abstract generalizations concerning mankind from what he observes in a novel implies that he is automatically creating a distance between himself and the material of the novel.

The danger inherent in the purposeful alienation of the reader is the possibility of creating too much distance between him and the subject. Cela uses five techniques to isolate the subject of his novel from the common experience of his audience. It is possible that what many critics have felt to be wrong with Cela's novel is that he has overalienated the reader's emotions and, consequently, his interest. It will soon become evident that Cela has turned away from the drastic devices for alienating the reader, employed in *Mrs. Caldwell*, substituting a more moderate approach that has been singularly practicable and successful.

6

La catira:

AN EXPERIMENT WITH THE ETHIC ARCHETYPE

La catira[1] was written by Cela upon the request of the Venezuelan government. Although the novel was written in Palma de Mallorca, Cela spent a few months in Venezuela in preparation for the task. The author received a handsome sum of money from the Venezuelan government for his effort, but his earthy picture of life on the *llanos* did not endear either Cela or his novel to the Venezuelan people. The latter have the right to dispute Cela's sociology of Venezuela and the authenticity of the Venezuelan dialect featured in the work. However, even if we were to assume that *La catira* presents a false picture of Venezuela—and it seems that the issue has yet to be resolved—the novel would still remain a valuable contribution both to Cela's reputation and to the development of the novel in Spain.

In writing a novel inspired by the Latin-American locale, Cela has done more than write a regional novel from a foreigner's point of view. Many reviewers have compared Cela's novels to those of Valle-Inclán, and his apparent sadistic irony in the face of mankind's plight is reminiscent in many ways of both Valle-Inclán and Quevedo. Such a resemblance appears strengthened by *La catira,* which recalls Valle-Inclán's *Tirano Banderas,* set in Mexico. These commentators have tried to see in Cela's novels in general and in *La catira* in particular the direct descendant of the *esperpentos.*[2] Admittedly,

Cela's novel is no travel brochure, but it would be difficult to accuse him of distortion. The principal characters of the novel may be false in their sociological origins, but they never become caricatures. *La catira* is important primarily for its subject and for the ability that Cela shows in adapting his concepts of the novel to a foreign tradition. This chapter demonstrates Cela's approach to his foreign subject matter and the manner in which he establishes a Venezuelan archetype in the figure of Pipía Sánchez.

Plot

La Catira, which means *la rubia* in the Venezuelan dialect, is Primitiva Sánchez, known even after her two marriages as Pipía Sánchez. As the novel opens, don Filberto Marqués is preparing to receive the runaway Pipía, who has fled from the land of don Froilán Sánchez, her supposed father. Pipía and Marqués are being married when Sánchez and his men appear to reclaim Pipía. In the ensuing confrontation, Marqués is killed, and Pipía mortally wounds Sánchez. When the dust has settled, *La Catira* is legally wed, but still a virgin, and the mistress of two wealthy cattle ranches. However, she is unable to preside peacefully over her land until Aquiles Valle, the rebel cattle boss of the ranch held by her husband's maiden aunts, is killed. The following chapters describe the successful pursuit of Valle led by Juan Evangelista Pacheco. Part One ends with Pipía's decision to marry Pacheco.

Part Two is contemporaneous with the writing of the novel (1954). Pacheco has died, leaving a son. The several chapters describe Pipía's efforts to consolidate her holdings, which now include those of the aunts and those of Pacheco. Her one obsession is to give her son a gentleman's education and to inculcate in him a responsibility for the land, for she realizes that the land will outlive her and that she must leave it an heir and a proprietor. Pipía hires a governess from the United States for her son and sends him in the jeep to meet the new employee at the airport. The vehicle collides with a steer, throws its occupants, overturns, and burns. As the novel closes, *La Catira*, her son dead, contemplates her naked figure in the mirror and resolves to marry again, still hopeful that she can give the land a master.

La catira is a novel of epic proportions in which Cela provides an extensive panorama of the human activity necessary to support Pipía Sánchez' ambition. Yet, in the tradition of *La colmena*, Cela never wanders far from his principal objective: to describe the importance the land has in the lives of the *llaneros*. Pipía Sánchez, the frustrated mother, stands out as the symbol of man's attempts to come to terms and to harmonize with the *barro primitivo* that is the land.

Formal and Structural Considerations

FORMAL ELEMENTS

La catira's nine chapters are divided into two sections. The *Primera Parte*, entitled "Viento oeste, viento barinés," is subtitled "La guerra." The *Segunda Parte*, entitled "La garza en el cañabraval," is followed by the words "y la paz." Part One has five chapters, Part Two, four. The subtitles indicate both the scope of the novel and the link between the two parts. Although some fifteen or sixteen years separate the events related in the two large divisions of the novel, they are intended to be complementary facets of the same panorama. Aside from Pipía Sánchez' domination of the first and final chapters of the novel, which portray her innocence and eventual maturity, the internal structure of the novel is random in the sense that there is no apparent patterning. Like *La colmena, La catira* consists of isolated narrative units. Any of the 133 units is only incidentally and only very occasionally dependent upon the two that enclose it. The principal formal difference that distinguishes Cela's use of the autonomous narrative unit in *La colmena* and in *La catira* is that in the earlier novel chronology is significantly altered, while the narrative of the later novel develops in a straight line through the several units, a structure suited to the development of a plot. *La catira* has a story to tell, a history to unfold. Although at times the narrative seems to go on unfruitful tangents, the digressions do not disturb the essential single-mindedness of the narrative. In one way or another, each of the individual narrative units may be directly related to Pipía Sánchez.

La catira makes abundant use of the narrative aside. Indeed, the short narrative sketches are ideally suited to the aside. Such asides further the narrative to the extent that they provide a social and ethical background for the principal concern of the novel. Pipía Sánchez and her blind desire to become one with the land and to give it a master form the foreground. The presence of the land and its miscellaneous inhabitants — both those who work for the land and those who work against it — are necessary to support the characterization of the principal figure of the work. In this way, we can justify from a purely formal point of view the long digression that occupies Chapters II through IV (the middle three chapters of the five that make up Part One), in which Juan Evangelista Pacheco, Pipía Sánchez' representative and future husband, is pitted against Aquiles Valle, the malevolent and perverted *caporal* who is attempting to usurp *La Catira's* control of the land. It is a violent and grisly man hunt, ending in Valle's death at the hands of the *caribera*. The digression is important within the structure of the novel for its affirmation of Pipía Sánchez' inherent right to and the implacable immutability of the land. Chapter IV, which describes Valle's unpleasant demise, concludes with the words, "En el horizonte se pintaron, rojas y elegantes, las nubes de la tarde. Lo mismo que el día del peleón del Turupial. El llano, a veces, varía poco, muy poco" (p. 172).

THE RETURN TO THE NOVEL FORM

Essentially, Cela has not abandoned the approach to the novel that begins in *Pabellón de reposo*, with its techniques for establishing an aloof perspective for the author and in turn for the reader. It is an approach Cela affirms in his subsequent two "social" novels through the application of the techniques for objectivity to the complex features of society. *La colmena* is Cela's most ambitious attempt to give the novel the illusion of being a human and social document. In *Mrs. Caldwell habla con su hijo*, the author refines his technique for creating objectivity and distance in the directions laid down in *La colmena*. The former represents a lapse in Cela's predominant interest in society as a whole and in the individual's role only incidentally.

La catira returns to the social context of man. Cela is basically an innovator. The often-seen statement that he has produced a whole series of novels, every one different, has become common critical coinage. Therefore, it is not impossible to imagine that in this novel Cela has striven to push the boundaries of his techniques to even further extremes in the search for new values and new modes in the novel, without altering his previous stand in regard to material and perspective.

Although Pipía Sánchez is ostensibly the focal point of Cela's narrative, it becomes increasingly obvious—and of this she herself is aware—that Pipía is little more than a touchstone for a higher reality. Despite her own powerful and dynamic personality, Pipía's ever-present desire to ensure a worthy male heir for the land results in an emphasis on the importance of the land as the cultural center of her society. Pipía stands out as an ardent spokeswoman for the reality of the geography and sociology by which she and her people must live. Her *caporales* and her *negras* are inarticulate. They recognize in their *misia*, however, the vocalization of the primitive code by which they must live as people of the land. The novel is successful in its affirmation of what the author believes to be the cultural patterns of the *llaneros* to the extent that Pipía Sánchez as an individual becomes aware of her place in and her responsibilities toward her society.

In this novel no clear distinction exists between the individual and his society. There is no Jamesian formula of a larger network of complex social interactions of which the individual, constantly foregrounded in the process, is continuously and laboriously becoming aware. In Cela's novel, Pipía Sánchez is already aware of these complexities, and her actions might be considered a step beyond mere recognition. In a certain sense Pipía Sánchez *is* her society. She is both a member of it and a quality that stands apart from it as its concrete embodiment. This dual role of a character effects the blurring between the class and the member. The confusion of the two aspects of the world of the novel, the separation of which was once considered a virtue, is no mere carelessness on the part of the author. Such procedure is part of a program for the novel that sees such a fusion as an absolute necessity.

THE COLLECTIVE UNCONSCIOUS AND CELA'S NOVEL

That the members of a society are joined together by bonds other than geographical and political is written boldly in the structure and in the narrative content of *La colmena.* The careless reader sees only chaos. Yet there is an order, a common denominator, that defines this Pandora's box of humanity. In spite of the multiplicity of his social contacts in the course of day-to-day living, a man always senses what his conduct is to be with every other man with whom he must deal. The subtlety and the variety of these conducts are what make *La colmena* so rich and at the same time weave a tight web of human interaction. In the last analysis, it is the latter that is the unique structure of the novel.

Much of the same apparent chaos and subtle interrelations constitute the background for *La catira.* The continually shifting patterns of the several narrative units shuffle and recombine a limited number of distinct personalities. Yet, there is a focal point in *La catira,* lacking in *La colmena,*[3] that extends beyond the limits of the interactions of individuals. This focal point is, of course, Pipía Sánchez, an archetypal character. The myth-orientation in the novel, derived from Jung's principles of the collective unconscious, emphasizes certain ideals or common denominators of a society. They may be positive values, such as those embodied in an epic hero, or, in twentieth-century terms, a militant and *engagé* crusader. Often they are negative values, indicative of the spiritual impoverishment of the common man. A novel can reflect these values or common denominators, either through the behavior patterns of many individuals acting together (choral novels), or by synthesizing them in the person of one central character (archetypal novels). If *La colmena* is basically choral in nature, *La catira* is essentially archetypal.

Examples of the novel of the collective unconscious are rare in contemporary Spain, but a strong current of Latin-American literature draws heavily, knowingly or otherwise, upon Jung's theories of anthropology. This current is one of the richest and most productive veins of Latin-American fiction.[4] The novels deal with man and his awareness of his place in society. Although in no way the exclusive property of leftist writers, the novel of the collective unconscious has flourished in Latin America, where manifold social problems and injustices abound. The socialist ethic of literature[5] has long proclaimed the necessity of the artist to respond to the problem of man and his society, and at a time when Latin America's writers are well aware of and concerned with the social problems of their respective countries, it is not surprising to find that their creative production, especially the novel, is attuned to the problems of man as a social being. These writers feel that they are under a strong obligation to create socio-cultural human archetypes embodying the values their creators feel their society is striving for and the problems it faces. In so endowing one individual with a cross-section of the ideals of his society at large, the authors appear to be heeding the following exhortation:

> Realismo [. . .] significa reconocimiento del hecho que la creación no se funda en una abstracta "media" como cree el naturalismo, ni sobre el principio individual que se disuelve en sí mismo y desvanece en la nada, sobre una manifestación exasperada de lo que es único e irrepetible. La categoría central, el criterio fundamental de la concepción literaria realista es el *tipo*, o sea aquella particular síntesis que, tanto en los caracteres como en las situaciones, unifica orgánicamente al género y al individuo. [En lo típico] se funden todos los momentos determinantes, hu-

mana y socialmente esenciales, de un cierto período histórico, y los representa en su máximo desarrollo, en la plena realización de sus posibilidades inmanentes, mostrándonos los rasgos característicos y la plenitud de un hombre y de una época.[6]

It is the particular synthesis mentioned that most characterizes these novels. Older novels often have characters who function in similar but allegorical rather than archetypal roles, for example, the novels of the *Doña Bárbara* stamp, with which Cela's own novel has, for obvious reasons, been compared.[7] The novels that may be grouped together under the heading of the collective unconscious rarely may be called allegorical, if one considers allegorical treatment the assigning to an entity a quality or qualities that it possesses beyond its normal attributes by virtue of its particular situation at a given moment. Rather, the heroes of these newer novels are more figural, possessing as part of their natural being qualities and significance that endow them with synthetic and typologic importance. Their personalities are archetypal in the sense that they characterize the history of their kind, its present moment, and the shape of its future.[8]

Cela is under no obligation, social or otherwise, to follow this trend in Latin-American literature when writing about Venezuela. That *La catira* shows a marked similarity to the novels of the collective unconscious, however, attests to Cela's desire to understand the nature of his subject matter in terms of the way a native might handle it and to Cela's phenomenal ability to adapt his novels to varying experimental modes.

The background to *La catira* is a choral one. Although no one has cast a *Censo de Personajes* for this novel, it is easy to imagine that the entries would be as numerous as is the one appended to *La colmena*. Despite the number of identifiable characters in *La colmena*, with the exception of a few outstanding ones all are given equal weight, since the majority of the narrative units highlight one or another of these characters at the expense of the others. Such is not the case in *La catira*, where roughly half of the narrative units are given over to the dialogue of miscellaneous and secondary characters. The arrangement of the novel is a continuous alternation between narrative units that deal with one of the principal characters and narrative units that deal with several of the secondary characters.

Although Cela exercises an evident and absolute control over his novel in accord with his novelistic principles, through the medium of certain aesthetic techniques, he is able to give his novel a poetic quality lacking in his other works. This poetic quality results from the stylistic elements, discussed by Olga Prjevalinsky,[9] and from the characteristics of the novel that Paul Ilie has identified as responsible for a narrative rhythm.[10]

The background, both choral and poetic, is characteristic of the type of novel under consideration and harmonizes with the intent to create a mythic pattern of reality. It is against this background that Cela places the principal characters whose personalities articulate the theme of the work — Pipía Sánchez, Juan Evangelista Pacheco, and Aquiles Valle.

Pipía Sánchez and Juan Evangelista Pacheco together reveal the influence of the spirit of the land and the responsibility the individual feels toward it. Pacheco is seen by Pipía as the means by which she, the Mother, will provide the land with a master. It is Pacheco who represents Pipía in those areas of activity that are closed to her as a woman, such as leading the armed posse against the renegade Aquiles Valle.

Valle is the antithesis of the virtues represented by Pacheco and Pipía, and it is significant that he is a sexual pervert referred to as *Moquinga*, the devil incarnate of the *llanos*. His death and the restoration of peace are decidedly optimistic notes in the novel.[11] It would not do to minimize the importance of Valle, in view of the several chapters devoted to his flight (Chapter II, III, and IV). Valle's disregard for the responsibility of man toward the land serves to place Pipía in relief.

Once Pipía has defeated Aquiles Valle, she sets about realizing her dream. Unlike the characters in *La colmena* and unlike many other mythic archetypes, Pipía Sánchez is fully aware of the role she is called upon to play. She affirms her position time and time again to those who would dissuade her from the heartbreaking and thankless goal she has set for herself:

> —Sí, negra . . . Tóos lo tenemo que entendé . . . La tierra quea, negra . . . La tierra quea siempre . . . Manque los cielos lloren, durante días y días y los ríos agolpen . . . Manque los alzamientos ardan, güeno, y mueran abrasaos los hombres . . . Manque las mujeres se tornaran jorras, negra . . . [. . .]—Hasta que el mundo reviente e la viejera, y el mundo ta entoavía finito, la tierra tié que se e la mesmitica sangre que la apaciguó. (pp. 356–57)

Pipía's efforts have not been in vain, for she has managed to communicate her feelings to the *pioná*, which fully understands them:

> Por el llano corrió el runrún de que la catira vendía.
> —La catira no pué vendé, cuñao, si la catira vende, güeno, la catira se muere e la pena . . . La catira ha puesto tóa su sangre en la tierra, vale, tóa su sangre y la sangre e tóa su gente . . . La Pachequera, cuñao, es como una cestica e sibisibe toíta rebosá e sangre . . . La sangre no es como el agua, cuñao, la sangre se pega duro y tarda en borrase . . . La sangre que se bota a la tierra, cuñao, no se pué comprá porque quema la mano . . . La catira tié que ejá su sangre, cuñao, onde ta su sangre . . . La catira es como la garcita que cae en el cañabraval, compae, que tié que resistí, pues, íngrima y sola, manque la soledá le pese, porque tié quebrá el ala y ya no pué levantá el güelo . . . Y la catira, cuñao, ¡no lo piense!, manque pudiera volá e su tierra, no lo haría . . . La catira no pué juí e la tierra que pacificó . . . La catira no juntó la tierra, cuñao, pa dirse e ella. ¿Sabe? (p. 351)

Although Pipía Sánchez is no dehumanized symbol, she does not appear as an individual, independent of her role as the mistress of the land. Pipía is very much alive, with a unique and vivid personality. Nevertheless, as a person she is unable to exist except in terms of the immediate surroundings with which she identifies completely. Pipía Sánchez is an archetype of her own free will, and it is in retrospect that we see her as an archsymbol of the land. She dominates the novel, and the narrative events always lead back to her and to her overriding preoccupation with her mission. For this reason we may speak of *La catira* as an archetypal novel despite its many choral elements.

Whether the reader can appreciate it or not, Cela's novel must be seen as a system of recurring narrative patterns, with Pipía Sánchez standing out as the focal point. An interpretation of *La catira*'s thematic intent must take into account the role which she plays in the structure of the novel. At least one critic has recognized this fact:

> [. . .]Pipía Sánchez. Una mujer aparte, que guarda en sí misma buena parte del secreto que la novela viene a comunicarnos: esa corza, esa loba, ese tigre, esa mujer atormentada, esa perentoria constancia luchando con lo efímero sobre la misma tierra. Desde ahora, una de las más fascinantes mujeres de la literatura universal.[12]

NOVELISTIC PERSPECTIVE

Once one has established that Pipía Sánchez is the focal point of both the narrative and the theme of *La catira*, two problems arise concerning her relationship with both the author and the reader: what the various technical perspectives of the novel are, and to what degree the effect of audience-distancing is present. The following discussion is divided into two parts. The first will deal with *La catira* and with the problem of perspective and alienation; the second will deal with *La catira* and the principles of the collective unconscious in terms of the perspective of the novel.

As in all of his novels, Cela exercises complete control over the presentation of the narrative content of *La catira*.[13] The author's penchant for leaving the reader with the feeling of his omnipresence has been discussed previously, particularly with regard to *Pabellón de reposo*. Although in *La familia de Pascual Duarte* Cela attempts unsuccessfully to camouflage his existence, beginning with his third novel, while he is not prominent as a separate entity, he is ever present as the only possible source for many of the novels' characteristics. The novels all contain a level of authority that has been interpolated between the reader and the subject matter. This level is either an omniscient layer or, as in *Mrs. Caldwell habla con su hijo*, a series of devices for alienation that must be attributed to someone other than Mrs. Caldwell.

In *La catira*, the use of a narrator is one of the techniques for alienation. Whether one attributes the narration of events to Cela or to a separately identifiable narrator whom Cela allows to speak, there is little doubt that someone external to the events being reported is, in a sense, editing them for our reception. While such an "editing" process, or selection, is present in every novel, it is especially prominent in *La catira* as an obvious novelistic procedure, particularly in view of the language of the novel and its rigidly patterned structure.[14] The rigid patterns characterize the construction not only of individual phrases and sentences but of whole paragraphs and narrative units as well. It is often possible to reduce entire sections to a series of repetitive linguistic structures. The effect is a calling of the reader's attention to the language with the result that he may become so involved in it that he loses the theme.

Ilie sees an imitation of primitive language as central to the intent of the novel: "En *La catira*, Cela ha producido una novela [«primitivista»] cuyos elementos son característicos de la literatura y la existencia primitivas."[15] Whether Ilie's statement concerning Cela's desire to imitate the stylistic characteristics of primitive language is accurate or not depends upon one's definition of *primitive*, and whether rigidly formal syntactic structures in noncasual literature are sufficiently unique to primitive languages to be recognized as a primitivist imitation when used in the noncasual writings of "nonprimitive" languages. The language of *La catira*, in terms of structure (not of vocabulary or of orthographic representation of local phonology), is sufficiently artificial and non-standard for the reader to suppose the presence of a heavy hand upon the narrative. In short, the novel does not happen, either through a narrator or through our accidental observation of a set of occurrences. A strong external control is manifest in the exaggerated language of the novel. The syntactic structures of *La catira* come to represent the predominant elements of alienation of the reader. When the latter is forced to see the "reality" of the novelistic world through a grid of artificiality, his identification with and sympathy toward that world are considerably dulled. It stands at a distance, and in order to be fully in tune with it the reader is obliged to consider as normal for himself the only direct manifestation he has at hand: its language.

Dialect is a second aspect important in creating alienation, although not to the same extent as the syntactic structures, which represent a true innovation on Cela's part. The use of local dialect in literature in the Spanish language, while noticeable, has never caused any real problem of comprehension. Despite the richness and variety of local Spanish and its frequent literary use, every literate speaker is capable of recognizing and understanding a certain undefined norm or common denominator of the language. If the novelist follows that norm in his works, he can be understood in every corner of the Spanish-speaking world. It is for this very reason that Cela's novel would have created a furor, even if everyone were to accept the authenticity of the *venezolanismos* he uses. The issue is not so much the authenticity of the Venezuelan dialect employed in *La catira* but that it was used at all by a non-Venezuelan. It is true that Cela's novel would be understood with little difficulty by any speaker of Spanish, but he would be overly aware of its linguistic peculiarity. Such an awareness increases in proportion with the distance between the reader and the dialect involved. While the language of the novel is quickly understood, no reader is going to mistake Cela's Spanish as normal to literate or noncasual situations, one of which is the printed word. At the same time it is evident that, despite the fact that *La catira* was written on commission from the Venezuelan government, Cela's largest reading public is in Spain, a country far removed from the language of the novel. Although Cela is read abroad—several of his works were originally published in Mexico—it is only natural that he is best known at home.

This leads to the second point in the discussion of Cela's techniques for alienation, the relation that exists between the content of the novel and the experiences of the reader. With the possible exception of Venezuelans and some other Latin Americans, the majority of the readers of the novel are going to be unfamiliar with the social and cultural problems it presents. The more literate the reader is—and the novel is written for a literate audience that can appreciate Cela's stylistic innovations—the further he is likely to be removed from the reality of the land. When such a situation exists, the author is called upon to create an empathy between his subject matter and the reader that would not otherwise be present as part of the previous experience of the latter. Witness the case of the writers of the Generation of '98 who, as urbanites, felt called upon to create a feeling for the land in both themselves and in their readers. Cela's problem is a particularly complex one, for he has not attempted to make his subject more familiar either to the Latin-American reading audience or to his much larger body of Spanish readers, many of whom have no concept whatever of life in the Americas. Cela chooses, instead, to forego the responsibility of approximating his readers to the theme of his novel, and the result is a severely maintained distance.

Another way in which Cela creates distance between his subject and the reader is by making much of his subject distasteful. This he accomplishes through both characterization and description. This aspect of the novel has been attributed to *tremendismo*, although Cela himself has repudiated such a literary category. Cela's insistence upon the "primacy of instinct"[16] and the anticivilization motif running through his novel, in addition to these other characteristics, do little to promote reader-identification.

Cela's use of a narrator who is more closely identifiable with the world of the novel than with the world of the reader contributes further to alienation of the reader. Whether or not the narrator is indeed Cela is beside the point. The importance of the narrator of *La catira* is his complete understanding of and identification with his material and the manner in which he presents it. Thus, while the qualifications of "naïve," "simple," "unlettered with undoctored speech," "perfect imitation of the primitive subject" are aptly applied to the narrator, they cannot be used to say that he is not Cela. Cela, as the narrator Camilo José Cela, is all too capable of deliberately assuming a primitivist approach.[17]

Since the narrator is the source of the content of the novel, he creates distance primarily by means of language. However, consider as well the implications of the following passage:

> La catira Pipía Sánchez, para matar sus ocios y dar rienda suelta a sus energías, ordenó unas reformas en Potreritos. La catira Pipía Sánchez estaba triste y algo más delgada, quizás. La catira Pipía Sánchez estaba, también, hermosa, inútilmente hermosa.
>
> —¿Inútilmente hermosa, catira?
>
> —¡Guá, éjese . . . !
>
> A la catira Pipía Sánchez, el sol y el aire del llano no le quitaban la palidez. La catira Pipía Sánchez, en todo era muy señorita.
>
> —¿Qué hubo, catira, e aquel coló e rosa e la ribera que te pintaba la cara?
>
> —¡Guá, éjese ahora . . . !
>
> La catira Pipía Sánchez, sobre el potro *Chumito*, se fué a dar un paseo hasta el Turupial. (p. 151)

The reader has no evidence that Pipía's interlocutor is anyone but the narrator, and he can only assume that it is the narrator himself who is teasing Pipía. Since the narrator is not part of the story, either as a principal or as a minor character, it is noteworthy that he is able to break at will the autonomy of his narrative in this way. The effect is of being left out of the narrator's game. The reader is unable to predict when he is witnessing the reality of the world of the novel as an autonomous unit, reported faithfully but indifferently by the narrator as he supposedly observed it, and when it is a fabrication of the narrator that he evokes and interrupts at his pleasure. The impression that the story is the exclusive province of a narrator who is not always willing to share it fully with his audience derives principally from the fact that the reader cannot separate his source of information from the information itself. Cela's approach to the foibles of the human personality is much the same in both *La catira* and *La colmena*. Yet, because of the sharp separation that exists in the latter novel between the narrator and his subject, the subject is not alienated from the audience as it is in *La catira*. This remains the most characteristic distinction between two novels that are very similar in technique and structure.

The second most prevalent practice of the narrator is the juxtaposition of passages that clash violently, creating an irony unfavorable to the reader:

> El amigo de don Juan Evangelista se llamaba Chachango Chávez y era tan fino que no pronunciaba la *che*. Los que no pueden decir la *erre*, suelen llamarse Roque Ruiz, o Ramón Ramírez, o Roberto Rodríguez y suelen, también, pasarse la vida hablando de perros sin rabo, de revoluciones rusas o de rascas de ron, de morrocotudas rascas de ron. Esas son las cosas que pasan.
>
> —Aquiles Valle tié que andá muy cerca e pu acá. La gente, cuñao, no se quié entrepiteá, y pa mí que jace e lo más bien, peo a Aquiles Valle lo han señalao rejendiendo pal norte, pué se que pa Apurito, pué se que pal Samán. Aquiles no pué andá lejísimos, güeno, pa mí como que se lo van a topa antes de lo que piensan. . . . (pp. 146–47)

The first passage is humorously irrelevant. The second concerns the pursuit of Aquiles Valle, who, just two pages before, has killed and raped a young man.

If the identification is accurate of these elements of *La catira* as techniques on the part of the author to achieve aesthetic distance, it is necessary to reconsider the collective unconscious at this point. The collective unconscious has often been identified as an approach employed by those novelists who, for external but nevertheless valid and important reasons, have as their goal the sympathetic identification of the social reality of man, usually a social reality of the lower classes. They are socialistic novels in the best sense of that ideology. For several significant reasons, it cannot be said that Cela's novel demonstrates this aspect of the collective unconscious in any way, despite his use of the basic characteristics of this approach to reality.

In the first place, *La catira* offers the reader little opportunity to identify with either its characters or its theme. This does not mean that the subject is incomprehensible or uninteresting. It means merely that the subject exists beyond the immediate experience of most readers and that the form of the novel offers little compensatory *rapprochement*. The novel does not deal with the social realities of life on the level of the reading audience, something for which the typical novel of the collective unconscious strives. The socialistic ethic in the novel concerns itself with the realities of life, both circumstantial and emotional. Cela has accepted this exigency, as have indeed most modern novelists. What Cela has refused to do is to suppose that the novel must deal with the immediate reality of the reader and that the reader must necessarily assume for the duration that the circumstances of the novel are his own. It is this latter assumption that is almost axiomatic for the majority of the Latin-American vanguard in the novel. This fact explains also why novelists have taken so enthusiastically to the possibilities offered by the mythic approach to literature. Their human types, if Jung's theories are correct, offer the masses (that is, the audience of the novel) a human prototype whom they can unconsciously admire and with whom they can unconsciously identify. The "heroes" of these novels, in having as the basis of their personality all the common denominators of their culture, are raised by the novelist to the status of ethical and social leaders. This has been widely done before, and such a procedure is not the exclusive property of the Latin-American novel, although it is one of the dominant characteristics of that novel at this moment.[18] There is little doubt that Pipía Sánchez is presented in terms of one of these ethical heroes. The values she symbolizes are positive values. While they are not necessarily the best possible values from a social and economic point of view, there can be no denying their dynamic qualities. And, too, Pipía is in general favorably presented by Cela. At least she is not negatively presented. How, then, does *La catira* fail to involve the reader emotionally? The answer lies primarily in the nature of the circumstances surrounding Pipía Sánchez' world. The reader must bear in mind that she is fighting an apparently losing battle against the opposing forces of her society, and at the end of the novel she has only her spirit to keep her going and little in the way of demonstrable success. Cela provides her world with grisly and savage violence and employs a set of rhetorical devices that unconsciously distract the reader.

If Ilie is right in saying that Cela has written a primitivist novel about a microsociety with primitive values caught in a world in which primitive cultures, no matter how intrinsically appealing they may be, are doomed to eventual absorption by the forces of civilization, then it is no wonder that the reader can work up little empathy with the world of the novel as a whole. The values are powerful and appealing; the reality is sordid and unattractive. It is the unromantic vision that prevails, tempered by Pipía Sánchez' determination to continue the pursuit of her ideal in the face of almost certain failure.

There is one final argument against identifying Cela's intent in *La catira* too closely with that of his Latin-American contemporaries in the novel. For many there still remains, and will probably always remain, the nagging doubt as to the authenticity of the novel in terms of the external reality of Venezuela. Granted, faithfulness to an external reality is not a criterion for the novel as long as it is internally credible. However, since the novelists who use the collective unconscious as an approach to reality feel that they must be authentic to an external set of facts, the possibility that Cela gives a total, or even partial, falsification of Venezuela should serve quite effectively to separate *La catira* from those Latin-American novels with which it bears an otherwise marked thematic and technical affinity.[19]

7

Cela's Recent Fiction:

A COMMITMENT TO THE NEW NOVEL

AFTER a lapse of seven years, *Tobogán de hambrientos* appeared in 1962, Cela's first novel since his election in 1957 to the elite Royal Spanish Academy. Recently, *Garito de hospicianos* (1964) and *La familia del héroe* (1965) have appeared. These two works follow a significant pause in creative activity as far as the novel is concerned and represent a marked maturity in Cela's procedure as a novelist.

Cela's two preceding novels, *Mrs. Caldwell habla con su hijo* and *La catira*, have not had the success and acclaim that one is sure their author would have desired for them. *Mrs. Caldwell* is strictly an experimental novel that exaggerates alienation of the reader to the breaking point; *La catira*'s intrinsic characteristics guarantee controversy. In many eyes the two novels document a weakening in Cela's command of the genre, a weakening occasioned by unwarranted technical risks. Meanwhile, *La colmena* has stood as a sort of beacon for Cela's fiction, the one novel to which most critics turn with the admiration reserved for a mature and accomplished piece of writing. Although there has been much room for disagreement, Cela's statements on the novel both at the time of *La colmena*'s publication and afterward make sense as a program for the novel. Their effective utilization in the novel testifies to their intrinsic good sense. A workable program and the ability to put it into effect were considerations in *La colmena*'s success.

Tobogán de hambrientos

Cela has in many ways returned to the workable program of *La colmena* in *Tobogán de hambrientos* while preserving many of the characteristics of the new novel.[1] He has checked the exaggerated tendencies of his two previous novels, particularly the devices for audience-alienation. He has brought to *Tobogán de hambrientos* many of the stylistic devices most noticeable in *La catira*, and the language of this, his seventh novel, is undeniably Cela's best effort. *Tobogán de hambrientos* may be less of a novel than any of Cela's previous works, but at the same time it reaffirms all of his concepts of the novel.

But one wonders about the course Cela's fiction will take in the future. The doom of the novel prophesied by so many critics is difficult to accept. If the Armageddon of the novel does draw nigh, it is because the novel as a formal outlet for artistic experience no longer answers the needs of the artist. It is too early to say that Cela has abandoned or "destroyed" the novel as a means for expressing his creative activity in the realm of narrative prose fiction. One might say that Cela sees what he agrees to call the novel as a literary vehicle which for him has neither formal nor structural a priori limitations. The novelist defines the novel by the act of construction, and the novel in turn is called upon to acknowledge its oneness with the author.

As does *La colmena*, *Tobogán de hambrientos* bears an external and verifiable resemblance to the sociological reality of Madrid, served up to the reader under the guise of a documentary by an ever-present author who leaves no doubt as to the provenience of what we are reading.

Tobogán de hambrientos has little plot, either on the level of the novel as a whole or on the level of its various narrative units. Cela's primary interest is to describe the behavior of men in certain situations. Description implies that action has already occurred and that the task of the author is one of creating the essence of the situation. As opposed to novelistic observation, which records real or hypothetical reactions of men for purposes of later commentary, description is biographic in nature. The narrative units of Cela's novel have a rigid and well-defined structure, and each serves to sketch the personality of one individual or of a group of individuals. Rarely do these individuals do anything; occasionally they speak to each other, their dialogue corroborating what the author has already said about them. Either plot as the unifying thread of a novel does not exist, or plot is life itself as a system of human interactions. Only this latter system of correspondences gives *Tobogán de hambrientos* cohesion.

FORMAL ELEMENTS

Tobogán de hambrientos consists of two parts. Each part is divided into one hundred unnumbered narrative units with short identifying titles. Part One (*Primer Tiempo*) is subtitled "Uno, Dos, Tres, Cuatro, Cinco . . ."; Part Two (*Segundo Tiempo*) is called "Cinco, Cuatro, Tres, Dos, Uno." These titles indicate two essential characteristics of the novel: form and time.

The first hundred narrative units present the interrelations and characterize the personalities of a group of people, numbering one hundred, who are seen in the order 1, 2, 3, 4, 5, . . . 100. There is no prescribed plan for progression from one individual to another; it happens as if of itself. Everyone knows or is related to someone else, and the discussion of one person leads naturally into the discussion of another: his brother, his friend, his sweetheart, his father, his neighbor, all of whom in turn are linked to other members of the human complex. Following closely the procedure of the new novel in substituting pattern for plot, Cela's work is reminiscent of the conversation of a backyard gossip who subtly and effortlessly moves from one person to another.[2]

The second hundred narrative units present roughly the

same individuals in reverse order, 100, . . . 5, 4, 3, 2, 1. Although a given individual may figure in several narrative units, two units related from one part to the other serve as a point of departure for tracing the complex relationship an individual has with the rest of mankind. There is no time sequence in either part and no temporal relationship between the two separate parts. While incidents of cause and effect may be cited, the novel presents two separate and not necessarily related moments in the state of affairs of a given set of human correspondences. In this respect, *Tobogán de hambrientos* is similar in form to *Pabellón de reposo*. However, in *Pabellón de reposo* the web of human relationships is not a consideration, and the formal elements are mechanistic and quite obvious. In *Tobogán de hambrientos* the multiplicity of individuals and the complexity of their relations with each other are such that the reader need not be aware of the author's mathematical mold. There is no predicting the shape a particular set of relationships will take even in the corresponding units of the two parts. The formal structure of the novel exists solely for the purpose of defining the extent of the narrative. Since the novel ends with the same individuals with which it began, *Tobogán de hambrientos* constitutes a circular narrative. Although not so circular as *Finnegan's Wake*, Cela's novel nevertheless achieves the delimitation of a segment of society that, if it were not for the external imposition of the form, would have an infinite extension. Cela justifies the formal elements of *Tobogán de hambrientos* on the following grounds:

> En estas páginas de hoy, el esqueleto que las sustenta es de culebra. No es mía la culpa de la afición que tengo (y que sí reconozco como mía) a coleccionar esqueletos dispares. Este *Tobogán de hambrientos* quizás no sea una novela para los legalistas de la preceptiva, aquellos que sueñan con matar a la literatura para ver si se está quieta de una buena vez y se deja estudiar con sosiego. A ellos quisiera rogar que inventaran un nuevo género (o una nueva denominación, que lo anterior sería demasiado pedir) o que, alternativamente, se decidieran a sentenciar

que este libro mío no tiene nada que ver con la literatura. supuesto tampoco improbable.

Tobogán de hambrientos pudiera clasificarse como cuento larguísimo, si admitiéramos que el substantivo y el adjetivo no se destruyen y neutralizan recíprocamente. La idea inicial de estas páginas brotó de mi pensamiento de que en esta vida todo está ligado y concatenado de forma que no queda jamás ni una sola pieza suelta; todas las cosas tienen un número – dijo, hace ya la mar de años, Filolao. El ejemplo de las cerezas es muy socorrido aunque, de paso, quizás ahora nos resulte tambíen insuficiente: los hombres y sus acaeceres están mucho más ligados entre sí que las rabilargas y arracimadas cerezas del frutero. (pp. 16–17)

The reader finds it difficult to keep in mind the hundred sets of intimate and intricate relationships of the characters of the novel. It is unnecessary that he do so, for little would be gained in the way of insight into their personalities and their doings. Rather, the novel's structure corresponds to what Cela feels is the natural pattern of life. His book is a potentially endless stream of individuals taken from his own experience with life, and its structure is one reasonable way of giving unity and coherence to such a collective presentation.

Theoretically it would be possible to add a *Tercer Tiempo* to the novel, reviewing the characters in the order 1, 2, 3, 4, 5, . . . 100, without exhausting the descriptive potential of their personalities. An infinite number of times would be admissible, first in one direction and then in the other. Yet, Cela has closed the cycle of his novel by means of the suicide of Florencio Basilio Pérez, the first character presented, thus imposing a natural boundary on his narrative. While Florencio is not the only person to die in the course of the novel, his suicide imposes a closing finality. Cela's declared intention of portraying the spiritual bankruptcy of these individuals has at that point been accomplished.[3] Although we cannot speak of the novel as having ended, the circle of interrelationships has been deftly closed, and the resulting totality is tantamount to a further narrative boundary.

COMPARISON WITH LA COLMENA

Perhaps what most reminds the reader of *La colmena* is Cela's manner of selecting and presenting his characters. The earlier novel proclaims its interest in the average man and in depicting the circumstances of his life. In order to meet this end, the author draws upon an almost limitless range of individuals, bringing relatively few of them together in narrative units that constitute revealing circumstances for their own self-portrayal. The common denominator of the novel is their situation in life and the overshadowing leitmotiv represented by Martín Marco's errant existence. *La colmena* is a circumstantial novel in the very miscellany of its content.

The contents of *Tobogán de hambrientos* are equally miscellaneous. Yet Cela has managed to marshal them into a tightly knit pattern of cause-and-effect relationships that gives the lives of the characters, if nothing more, a context of mutual acquaintanceship. The society of *Tobogán de hambrientos* is essentially a closed society from which both reader and author are excluded; they have no contextual relevancy to that society, and there is no place to fit them in without destroying the artificial but omnipresent balance of the structure of the novel. The result is an alienation much more subtle than Cela has attempted before, but one that is just as effective. Cela is present in his novel as the source of the narrative. However, he maintains his distance from the narrative, careful to assure the reader that he is its transmitter and not its creator. At one point he answers a question from the supposed audience:

> — ¿Y quién le mandó bañarse?
> — ¡Ah, no sé! Yo me limito a informar.
> — Tiene usted razón, dispense. (p. 230)

Such exchanges punctuate the narrative. Among other functions, they serve to isolate the author as an outside agent reporting what he has seen, heard, or been told.

The underlying structural link between any two narrative units of the novel serves to make each one stand out more from its neighbor than do the randomly joined units of *La colmena.* Each unit of *Tobogán de hambrientos* is of equal importance, and the structural link joins them without effacing their basic autonomy. They are two hundred character sketches, and each one may stand alone, since its relation to the others is more causative than narrative. A few story lines cross the boundaries of narrative units, but the story is never of any real importance, and nothing is lost if it is ignored. As a consequence, Cela's seventh novel gives the impression of being a twentieth-century *Generaciones y semblanzas.* Individuals and individual psychology are stressed, but the pertinence of the individual to the whole is never ignored. This is less the case in *La colmena,* where the hive effect of the choral atmosphere is an ever-present aim of the novel. Indeed, for this very reason Martín Marco, who is of little intrinsic interest, stands out merely because of the greater number of his appearances against the backdrop of the others.

Like *La colmena, Tobogán de hambrientos* is concerned with life in its rawest and most elemental of social forms. Cela's statement in the *Prólogo* to his novel expands on his statements in the prologues to *La colmena*:

> Sólo una cosa sé: la literatura es la vida misma, no ya su crónica artística o emocionada, y sólo otra cosa intuyo: vestir a la literatura con chaquetas y pantalones de confección — e incluso con chaquetas y pantalones lujosos y a la medida — es vano porque la literatura, al final, sale por el arbitrario registro de la mala crianza y se baja los pantalones a destiempo o se presenta, ¡qué descaro!, con la chaqueta al hombro y el culo al aire. (p. 13)

In this respect, *Tobogán de hambrientos* shares *La colmena's* orientation toward life. The principal difference between the two novels is reduced to their respective presentational techniques.[4] Although Cela has striven for the illusion of objectivity and documentary distancing in *La colmena,* by its structure the later novel realizes these goals much more effectively. Despite Cela's avowed distaste for "literary trappings," there is much more artifice in his seventh novel than there is in his earlier works, their most distinctive formal characteristic being the disruption of any chronological unity. Chronological unity, however, is inseparable from the cause-and-effect pattern of the narrative itself. On the other hand, in a novel such as *Tobogán de hambrientos* not only are chronology and temporal considerations unimportant, but the novel has an external structure as well that gives form to the narrative, a pattern that may be described without reference to plot. Aside from other implications it may have, such a mechanical and patterned structure points to a belief that an external and formal unity for the novel is both feasible and advisable. Cela admits in the *Prólogo* that:

> La novela precisa de un esqueleto – usual o inusual, de hombre o de rana – que, en todo caso, cuadre a sus intenciones y tamaños. La novela, con frequencia, falla por falta o sobre de armazón, por desproporción con el andamiaje que la sustenta, lo que le acarrea debilidad o la convierte en un monstruoso osteoma. Una novela, si tiene cuerpo y hechuras de elefante, se viene abajo si la mantiene – y ni la mantiene siquiera – un esqueleto de conejo. En el caso inverso, esto es, en el ambicioso supuesto de que el propósito – el armazón – sea mucho más soberbio que la escasa carne de que disponemos para cubrirlo, la novela se queda en fantasmal osario, tendencia peligrosa. (p. 15)

THE POSITION OF THE AUTHOR

Of primary importance are the technical devices, external to the narrative content itself, that the author-narrator employs to support the fiction that he is reporting something for which he is not responsible.

One might argue that the distinctions Cela makes for reader, author, and content are hardly unique to *Tobogán de hambrientos* and that indeed they are basic to our concept of the novel as a literary form. While this point is well taken, it fails to differentiate between a priori theoretical assumptions about the novel and those assumptions that are contingent upon the form of a novel. We would all agree that there is an external reality, life, that is common to all men. We would also all agree that novelists draw upon the external reality as material for their novels. Furthermore, we would all agree that novels are written to be read by readers who are part of the external reality of the novel, that is, life. Since the *external* being of a novel is fixed and immutable, only the declared *internal* nature of its existence may be significant as a part of the novelist's literary invention.

Cela's novel has three well-defined internal levels. There is first the narrative itself, consisting of two hundred sketches. At random points, dialogue exchanges are interpolated that cannot be attributed to characters in the novel. At first the reader is inclined to think of them as exchanges between the author and his audience, especially because these interruptions often anticipate the reader's objections or questions on a particularly perplexing comment by Cela. However, one soon realizes that, while it is indeed a question of Cela speaking with his audience, that audience does not include the reader. Although not a general rule, Cela will occasionally identify his interlocutor by name and may even say a few words about him.[5] The reader is consequently relegated to a tertiary position from which he observes the author narrating an incident to an audience. The effect is similar to that of a television viewer watching a children's story hour, with the attentive youngsters gathered around the storyteller's feet. The story is told for their interest, and, although we are permitted to listen in, we are definitely left out of the inner group. Although Cela's ultimate objective in such a procedure is reader-distancing and the illusion of a documentary, the most immediate result for the reader is the ability to distinguish those portions of the novel that stand alone as the microsociety of the novel.

Once the microsociety of the novel has been identified for the reader, the author imposes upon it limitations he could not employ if both he and the reader were in agreement that the novel represented a witnessing of life by the reader rather than a secondhand reporting of it by the author. In effect, Cela's limitations consist of abolishing the cosmic boundaries of time and history.

Tobogán de hambrientos has defined for itself a beginning and an end, and in this way it differs substantially from Cela's other novels in which the terminal point is arbitrary. In *La familia de Pascual Duarte*, *Pabellón de reposo*, and to a certain extent in *Nuevas andanzas y desventuras de Lazarillo de Tormes*, the narrative ends because the manuscript source has been exhausted. Only in *La catira* and in the *Lazarillo* do there seem to be natural endings, based on the attainment of a narrative plateau. On the other hand, *Tobogán de hambrientos* and *La colmena* (and *Mrs. Caldwell* as well) end when and where they do for no justifiable reason other than that is where the author would have them end. It is interesting to note, nevertheless, that in these two narratively open-end novels, Cela has chosen to erect an external structural device in order to give the novels a finality they would not otherwise possess on the basis of narrative alone. In *La colmena* it is the sequence of events turning in upon itself; in *Tobogán de hambrientos* it is the circular geometric pattern.

This geometric pattern of *Tobogán de hambrientos* obviates to a large extent the possibility of a system of cause-and-effect relationships as the basis of any narrative. The almost necessary lack of a narrative makes temporal sequences of events superfluous and nonfunctional, and temporal considerations are subsequently of only the slightest importance in *Tobogán de hambrientos*. As in *Pabellón de reposo*, the reader observes a given set of human interrelationships embodied in a given narrative unit at the two different moments represented by their places in each of the two sections of the novel. Although there is no temporal unity within either part, as in *Pabellón de reposo*, any two corresponding sketches in the two parts necessarily constitute two separate moments; otherwise the incidents and occasional dialogue they describe would be identical, word for word, in both sketches.

Cela goes beyond this atemporality by the use of a few devices for negating time. One is the temporal overlapping of two corresponding sketches. For example, No. 6 (pp. 37–40) tells of the death of Miss Titbit. In Part Two, No. 6A (pp. 481–83), the narrative does not resume at this point, but backtracks. This procedure is evident in the majority of the narrative units that, therefore, cannot be put end to end but must be superimposed to interlock and form one set of data. The result is a body of information that cannot be assigned any significant and precise temporal limits.

The second device employed by Cela to destroy temporal relations between incidents and individuals consists of an ambivalence in the grammatical tenses used. Each narrative is supposed to have a relation to the two that precede and follow it, on the basis of human interaction and relationships. There is, however, no necessary equivalent temporal relationship, and the two units do not fuse in time along any given narrative thread. One example will suffice: No. 7 (pp. 40–42) deals with Paquita de Castro del Río; the time is past, and the verbs are preterite and imperfect. No. 8 (pp. 43–45) moves on to consider Paca Roldán, Paquita's mother; the time is present, and the verbs are present. This procedure is used frequently.

Tobogán de hambrientos' distinctive levels that separate the reader from the storyteller and his audience, in addition to the technique of the novelist for the suspension of temporal and historical boundaries, make the content of the novel a distinctly closed society. The world of the novel is one in which neither the author nor the reader is allowed to participate. The author cannot participate and at the same time stand back and observe society as clearly and as sardonically as his novel shows him able to do. It is taken for granted that Cela is a part of the society he describes.[6] On the basis of the internal assumptions of his novel he is marginal. This fact is reflected in the novel's insistence that the author is indeed standing away from his subject and commenting upon it to a third party.[7] From the opposite point of view, Cela affirms that the characters whom he is discussing are themselves unaware of the full nature of their personalities and circumstances:

> La Visitación Budia, la esposa del Sebas, es, sin ir más lejos, un asco.
> —Pero, ¿un asco del todo?
> —Sí, mi buen amigo, un asco de los pies a la cabeza. ¡Un verdadero asco!
> —¡Pobre!
> —Pues no, no crea; ella ni se da cuenta. (pp. 95–96)

Whatever the immediate effects of Cela's devices, they can be fully understood only within the broader framework of his attempt to achieve reader-alienation and an illusion of objectivity. Little need be said at this point to define the principle of reader-alienation. The discussions of the technique as it applies to both *Mrs. Caldwell* and *La catira* are equally applicable here.

One characteristic of *Tobogán de hambrientos* that distances the reader is the use of sketches that are more descriptive and biographical than they are narrative. In the great prototypes of the novel a series of incidents or a system of human interactions takes place, as if of its own accord. The reader is left to draw his own conclusions and to form his own judgments and opinions. In Cela's novel the author is always there, omnipresent and generally omniscient, giving us a summary of what has happened and only occasionally allowing the characters to speak for themselves. It is as if Cela were hovering over a tank of rare tropical fish, pointer in hand, singling out for the amusement of his audience the interesting features of his collection.[8] The reader is pushed back a step further to observe these proceedings, only infrequently seeing over the shoulders of Cela and his interlocutor. Such a procedure does not deprive Cela's novel of either authenticity or interest. Cela is a competent and perceptive reporter whose language alone holds the attention of the reader by its appropriateness and forthrightness. What is implied, however, is a different function for the novel; this function is, of course, Cela's belief in the documentary illusion of the novel.

Tobogán de hambrientos tends to reduce people to the status of objects. The characters and their respective personalities are tokens in Cela's portrayal of his society. No one individual is of any real importance.[9] Said differently, the elimination of any one character would not markedly alter the novel. Rather, of primary interest is the picture of mankind they form together. Cela has a tendency to treat his characters as so many movable pieces of humanity. This tendency is intensified by the abolition of the temporal and historical limitations that in other novels hold the characters in their places against the importunities of the author. Such is not the case in *Tobogán de hambrientos*; Cela is free to move them around at will, only imperceptibly limited by his own self-imposed structural design.

In distancing both himself and his audience (both fictional and real) from the subject at hand, Cela is able to indulge in a constant irony against his characters. For example:

> La Belencita Catarroja Trainera, alias Punching-ball (léase Punchinbol), tiene dos veces más fuerzas que el Cesarín; vamos, quiere decirse que es capaz de levantarlo — o de tumbarlo — con una sola mano. La Belencita Catarroja Trainera, alias Punchinbol, es profesora de cultura físcia, oficio que se le nota, ¡vaya si se le nota!, hasta en la manera de escupir. Cuando los dos eran pequeños, la Belencita le decía al Cesarín, que era más flaquito:
>
> — Cesarín, te echo un pulso, ¿quieres?
>
> Y el Cesarín, como es de sentido común, le decía que no. (pp. 54–55)

Cela goes on to describe how Punching-ball has written under the *nom de plume* of Simonne de Roche "una novela tremendista," which with various titles has been a finalist in several contests.[10] Irony of this sort is rampant in *Tobogán de hambrientos*. It is easy to say that the reader of the novel is unable to see his personality and his life on the same level with that of Punching-ball, *et al.* This is perhaps one of the most effective devices for reader-distancing, and Cela exploits it very effectively.

Cela's insistence on commenting upon the personalities of characters rather than allowing them to reveal themselves through their actions is so extensive in this novel that action as such hardly exists. This procedure is common enough in *La colmena*, where it often leads to irony when Cela's external commentary clashes with the spoken intentions of the characters. In *Tobogán de hambrientos*, Cela's commentary is a running exposition of human vanities, false pride, and egocentrism. It is only natural that the reader wonder what the novelist hopes to gain by such a technique, a technique that is in many respects anovelistic. Throughout his career Cela has come more and more to consider the novel a vehicle for commentary upon the human situation. Most of his novels are plotless, and even novels like *La familia de Pascual Duarte* and *La catira* demonstrate a preoccupation on the part of the author with the isolated analysis of human behavior. Although Cela's first novel stands alone in many respects, it shares basic affinities with the novels that follow. All of the novels considered in this study show Cela essentially interested in man as a set of human foibles. Whether he is cast in a mold that has no external point of reference (the introverted form of *Pabellón de reposo* and the new novel form of *Mrs. Caldwell habla con su hijo*) or whether it is one that gathers significance from the complex web of human society (the majority of Cela's novels), the exposition of men and their personalities is foremost in Cela's mind. Cela's more recent fiction points to a realization that man does not exist in a vacuum. This realization explains the mythic-cultural ties of Pipía Sánchez and the involved interrelations of *Tobogán de hambrientos*. Yet, when all is said and done, the description of the social background of the individual is of only minor importance.

Cela is not the first to come to this conclusion, but the difference for him is that man is man despite his social background. While it is true that he cannot be divorced from it, nor can he be seen out of context with it, his social background does not account for the nature of his personality. Where James's characters are children of their culture, Cela's characters are simply members of it. Commentators who see Cela's novels as no more than indictments of Spanish civilization are failing to see this difference.[11] Spain as a series of character-forming institutions does not exist in Cela's novel. If Cela gives a bleak picture of mankind, it is on the basis of the inherent, immutable, and universal "original sin" of mankind.[12] This is true not only of *Pascual Duarte* but of every novel Cela has written. Spain, with the exception of *La catira* and *Mrs. Caldwell habla con su hijo*, is little more than a geographic setting in Cela's novels. Therefore, Cela need not go to great lengths to establish the personalities of his characters, nor need he bother with a long-drawn-out Jamesian situation in which the individual reveals himself through his intercourse with other individuals. If Cela believes that all men, regardless of social or cultural background, exhibit basically the same human weaknesses, he may dispense with the traditional world of the novel. In addition, if Cela believes that the novelist's task is to expose the universal characteristics of mankind and not just of a few individuals, then he also may consider character sketches that retain the complex interrelationships of mankind as the only convenient form for the novel.[13]

Tobogán de hambrientos speaks for Cela's intimate hope for the novel: the illusion of a human document, fictional in detail and artistic in elaboration, reflecting the personal view of the author of the human soul. Because the novel is a personal document for Cela, he is able to insist upon reader-distancing as part of his desire for an emotional objectivity by which the reader, a man himself with all of the failings of mankind, is forced to stand back and observe the intense tragicomedy of his plight.

We may attribute the sporadic use of dialogue to the same desire. Usually we think of dialogue as an opportunity for the characters to reveal themselves. This is true only to a certain extent in Cela's novels. More often, the characters speak to provide support for Cela's description of them. This and the fact that often the dialogue interchanges in *Tobogán de hambrientos* are author-audience asides indicate that dialogue and the "real-life" situations it evokes are only an occasional convention tolerated by an author convinced that he knows his characters better than they know or can reveal themselves.

In his attempt to lay bare what he believes to be the human soul as it really is, Cela has recourse to many devices that guide the reader's judgment. These devices take the form not only of speaking for his characters, but also of an extensive network of asides that anticipate the reader's judgment of events and ensure that he reaches the proper conclusions:

> La Visitación Budia, la esposa del Sebas, tiene poca memoria y, a veces, se olvida de que el Esculapio no le resulta simpático.
>
> —No es mala persona, el pobre anda delicado de salud.
>
> Entonces la Visitación Budia, la esposa del Sebas, le recoge las colillas de Sebas, que le da, muy bien envueltas en un paquetito para que nadie las vea, los domingos al salir de misa.
>
> —Parece buena mujer, la Visitación.
>
> —No; la Visitación no es ni buena ni mala; lo que le pasa a la Visitación es que es olvidadiza. Las mujeres, tan pronto parecen buenas como malas, depende del viento que les sople en la memoria: si recuerdan, son malas; si no recuerdan, hasta se les puede hablar . . . , ¡eso va en suertes! (p. 97)

The last two paragraphs, an exchange between the reader and the author, constitute one instance out of many where Cela makes sure that the reader forms the right opinion. In these respects Cela is truly *deus ex machina.*

Cela's novel is a novel of people as individuals, and any attempts to analyze the thematics of the novel must do so on that basis. *Tobogán de hambrientos*, along with all of Cela's novels, with the possible exception of *Pabellón de reposo* and *Mrs. Caldwell habla con su hijo*, constitutes a paradox. It insists upon the social orientation of mankind. The very structure of the novel is a strong affirmation of the web of human relationships in which the individual is irrevocably caught. However, many readers fail to distinguish between society as a set of institutions that control man and society and as a congress of mankind that engulfs man. Mankind is cruel and senseless as well as usually depraved; the institutions of a society are merely by-products and manifestations of this truth. The prefatory quotation to *Tobogán de hambrientos* sets the tone of the novel and establishes early its interest in men as part of mankind: "Bien aventurados los Juan Lanas, los cabestros, los que lloran como Magdalenas, los incomprendidos, los miserables, los tontos de pueblo, los cagones, los presos: en el Evangelio de San Mateo se les consuela a todos" (p. 11).

Both the title of the novel and Cela's own statements in the Prologue establish the theme of spiritual hunger and starvation. At the same time, the technical devices that have been discussed point to Cela's ever-present desire that the reader understand what the novelist believes life to be, without becoming emotionally involved lest he be unable to appreciate it fully. Only in these terms are we able to understand how Cela gives such an intensely pathetic vision of mankind while seeming to distance his reader from it, at times through the use of the most jarring examples of irony. Cela's vision of mankind and his use of irony often approach the great works of the Renaissance. His neutrality and the neutrality he demands from his reader are summed up in the following reader-author aside:

> El Florencio Guadalán Mogón, alias Chaqueta, es muy considerado con su señora; trabajar no trabaja, eso es cierto, pero es muy considerado con su señora. Al Florencio Guadalán Mogón, alias Chaqueta, le fallan algunos resortes pero el no tiene la culpa: cada cual es como Dios lo hizo.
>
> —¿Y usted no cree que los hombres puedan tener arreglo, si se lo proponen?
>
> —¡Hombre, no sé! ¡Contra la naturaleza no se debe luchar! ¡La naturaleza es muy sabia y sabe muy bien lo

que se hace! ¡Los seres humanos somos como pigmeos al lado de la naturaleza!
— ¡Caray!
— Sí, amigo mío, lo que usted oye. (p. 124)

Very few authors are as explicit as Cela is in indicating their theory of the novel and exactly how they want their novels to be understood. Cela's novels are the result of his very utilitarian concept of the novel, and he is forthright in declaring its intentions. The reader may disagree with both Cela's theories and with his thematics, but it is only fair that he observe their explicit guideposts while reading Cela's novels.

*Garito de hospicianos and the Question of the Validity of the Novel**

Cela has always been leery of the novel, both in the sense of a well-defined literary genre with its own canon of formal regulations and in the word itself, putting in doubt the possibility of accounting for its applicability to the variegated and divergent examples of contemporary fiction. Only half in jest did he observe in the prologue to *Mrs. Caldwell habla con su hijo*:

> He coleccionado definiciones de novela, he leído todo lo que sobre esta cuestión ha caído en mis manos, he escrito algunos artículos, he pronunciado varias conferencias y he pensado constantemente y con todo el rigor de que pueda ser capaz sobre el tema y, al final, me encuentro con que no sé, ni creo que sepa nadie, lo que, de verdad, es la novela. Es posible que la única defnción sensata que sobre este género pudiera darse, fuera la de decir que «novela es todo aquello que, editado en forma de libro, admite debajo del título, y entre paréntesis, la palabra *novela*».[14]

Although one suspects that Cela is attempting to speak in his own self-defense against the often acerbic critic who has seen

* I express here my appreciation of the kindness shown by the editors of *Hispania* in permitting me to incorporate into this chapter these remarks, which appeared first as an article in that journal: *Hispania*, 49 (May, 1966), 244–49.

in his novels little to earn commendation and much to merit condemnation, what he has to say is interesting in its own right. It would be necessary to reproduce the entire prologue here in order to give an idea of Cela's self-evaluation. What emerges, however, is that up to and including *Mrs. Caldwell* Cela's novel has been dedicated to a constant trying out of various forms or modes of fiction in a search for the one that best suits him and the particular artistic exigencies of what he has to say concerning the human situation. One might add that it is a search which continues through Cela's subsequent novels.

At the same time that Cela has been undertaking this experimentation with the varying forms to which narrative prose fiction, because of its very nature, so lends itself, as the editor of one of Spain's most distinguished literary reviews[15] he has also been an outspoken critic of the traditional forms of the novel and the restrictions which self-appointed guardians of the integrity of the older forms of the novel would impose upon the creative artist. This interest on Cela's part may be traced back to his prologue to the first edition of *La colmena*:

> Mienten quienes quieren disfrazar la vida con la máscara loca de la literatura. Ese mal que corroe las almas, ese mal que tiene tantos nombres como queremos darle, no puede ser combatido con los paños calientes del conformismo, con la cata plasma de la retórica y de lo poética.
>
> Esta novela mía no aspira a ser más — ni menos, ciertamente — que un trozo de vida narrado paso a paso, sin retincencias, sin extrañas tragedias, sin caridad, como la vida discurre, exactamente como la vida discurre. Queramos o no queramos. La vida es lo que vive — en nosotros o fuera de nosotros — ; nosotros no somos más que su vehículo, su excipiente como dicen los boticarios.
>
> Pienso que hoy no se puede novelar más — mejor o peor — que como yo lo hago. Si pensase lo contrario, cambiaría de oficio.[16]

In the prologue to the third edition of *La colmena* Cela has become even more sure of the correctness of his views on literature and apparently more disillusioned with the possibility of even admitting lofty virtues in life and art. "La historia, la indefectible historia, va a contrapelo de las ideas. [. . .]Las ideas son un atavismo — algún día se reconocerá —, jamás una cultura y menos aún una tradición" (p. 15), he writes. By the time of the fourth edition (1962) Cela has chosen to use the word "historia" rather than "novela," although both still fall within the boundaries of fiction:

> A la historia — y éste es un libro de historia, no una novela — le acontece que, de cuando en cuando, deja de entenderse. Pero la vida continúa, aún a su pesar, y la historia, como la vida, también sigue cociéndose en el inclemente puchero de la sordidez. A lo mejor la sordidez, como la tristeza de la que hablábamos hace cinco años [en el Prólogo de la tercera edición], también es un atavismo. (p. 18)

The preceding quotation is contemporary to *Tobogán de hambrientos*, a novel which, although it has not been in print long enough to have stimulated any extensive body of criticism, has its own radical departures from the format of the traditional novel. Yet it is in its curious format that one would want to seek support for calling it literature and probably a novel. There is a definite structure and a definite progression of events (although difficult at times to follow), and the work culminates in the suicide of the individual who is first presented. What lies between the opening and closing sketches is the gently swaying sea of seething and teaming humanity that characterizes both *La colmena* and *La catira*. It is a sea of humanity that is neither pretty nor exciting. But it is a humanity that is vital and verisimile in the constant reciprocity of his behavior. The prologue to this novel, in the tradition of the prologues to *La colmena*, contains many interesting observations concerning *Garito de hospicianos* along with an explanation and possible justification for the format chosen. The prologue also contains the following thought-provoking words concerning Cela's running feud with the novel as an art form and its devoted defenders:

> Si supiera qué cosa es la novela, podría argumentar aquí el porqué estas páginas que hoy publico son — o distan mucho de ser — una novela. Pero acontece que, por más que pienso, ignoro — por lo menos de una manera científica y de fiar — cuáles son las lindes del género, quizás porque cada día que pasa veo más clara la convencionalidad — y consiguientemente, la ineficacia — de la clasificación que venimos usando para parcelar el monedizo suelo literario, el violento — y ende implacable — torrente de la literatura. Sólo una cosa sé: la literatura es la vida misma, no ya su crónica artística o emocionada, y sólo otra cosa intuyo: vestir a la literatura con chaquetas y pantalones de confección — e incluso con chaquetas y pantalones lujosos y a la medida — es vano propósito porque la literatura, al final, sale por el arbitrario registro de la mala crianza y se baja los pantalones a destiempo o se presenta, ¡qué descaro!, con la chaqueta al hombro y el culo al aire. Entonces, cuando la literatura se enseña de esa guisa, ¿qué es lo procede hacer? La respuesta es obvia: quemar los tratados de preceptiva y esperar a que a alguien se le ocurra una ordenación más lógica de las cosas. El que hoy la ignoremos, no significa que no exista. (*Tobogán de hambrientos*, pp. 13–14)

These and the words that follow affirm, in any case, Cela's desire to consider *Tobogán de hambrientos* literature and, more specifically, to consider it a novel.

It is interesting to note, however, that Antonio Fernández Molina has approached *Tobogán de hambrientos* from the point of view of its moral or didactic intent. The fact that the article appeared in Cela's own review may be taken as a tacit acknowledgment of the appropriateness of the ideas advanced. Fernández Molina's main point rests on his belief that, whereas many contemporary novels and their immediate predecessors have substituted for the hero of the eighteenth- and nineteenth-century novel the antihero of the first half of this century, Cela has substituted for both the "infrahero" whose principal characteristic, beyond the degree to which he is individual and personal, is the way in which, quite literally, he is a man of his own place and time. What is of immediate consequence is the way in which Cela sees this man's own place and time. The critic sees in Cela's novel an interest in the basically comic[17] and pathetic nature of man, not only of contemporary man, but of mankind in general. The venal nature of man is prime stuff for Cela's novels from *Lazarillo de Tormes* to the present one, and Fernández Molina indicates the way in which Cela maintains that the recognition of that venality is the first step in attacking it and perhaps in changing it:

> El mundo que nos retrata Cela no es ni puede ser sino el que conoce y padece a diario, el que también le afirma como hombre, como escritor y que a un tiempo le sirve de tormento y de espectáculo (él qué culpa tiene) entretenido. El escritor es ya un filósofo, un humorista y a esta alturas no se asusta de nada. Toma nota de la realidad, que es la verdad y nos ofrece una serie de tipos en los que podemos reconocernos y corregirnos.
>
> [. . .]Cela, deliberadamente, como un fotógrafo de pueblo, hace la fotografía de los elementos de una sociedad que presenta como ejemplo a corregir, no se burla de ella y si señala sus defectos es porque le obsesionan, porque los siente como algo muy suyo, de lo que se burla pero que sin duda no vería con buenos ojos que las burlas partieran de alguien que no participara del parentesco.[18]

Turning our attention to Cela's most recent book, *Garito de hospicianos*,[19] we are faced with an extremely perplexing and potentially embarrassing problem. One of the first things that strikes the critical reader is the lack of any similarity to narrative prose fiction, although there can be little doubt that this is literature, and very well-written literature, to be sure. One must either accept *Garito de hospicianos* as a further Celian mutation (or mutilation) of the novel, or play into the hands of the self-righteous critics by saying that now Cela has gone just too far. Or we may agree that it is not a novel, assign it to another category of literature, and proceed to explain why, while *Tobogán de hambrientos* is a novel, *Garito de hospicianos* is not. For purposes of discussion the last approach has been chosen, and an attempt to offer some justification for this opinion follows.

In the first place, Cela himself speaks in his prologue to *Garito de hospicianos* of either a literature that is an operation completely divorced from reality and dependent upon the novelist's a priori decisions as to the nature of the facts, or of a literature that is life itself—not the reporting of life, but its very essence:

> Los escritores, como cada hijo de vecino, vivimus de buscarle los tres pies al gato. El timo de la estampita y el del portugués, por ejemplo, nacen de la misma fuente que la novela de técnica más compleja y al día. Los escritores solemos resistirnos a admitir que esto es así pero, cuando logramos ordenar nuestra humildad, nos salta como un gazapo y ante nuestras narices la evidencia de la ruin cuna de la materia que manejamos: la vida, eso que — como los murciélagos — busca la penumbra para delatarse.
>
> [. . .]La literatura, pese a todas sus gratuitas idealizaciones, es un garito de hospicianos en el que todos los reclusos son pardos aunque griten como demonios y sin licencia de Dios ni de las autoridades.[. . .]
>
> Los hospicianos de la literatura, en su garito, silban canciones revolucionarias para llamar la atención de lectores y contribuyentes, mientras la policía, guiada por sus gratuitas delaciones (no siempre ciertas), los va fichando y estrujando uno a uno y sin que ninguno escape ni sueñe siquiera con escapar. Es tan elemental como cruel el juego — o el tejemaneje — de los títeres que agonizan en el garito hospiciano (pintándose las mejillas de arrebol y luciendo, a diario, la corbatita de los domingos). Lo que acontece es que nadie quiere decirlo porque todos prefieren el mísero *stato quo* de la literatura: el sepulcro blanqueado en el que se van pudriendo, sin pena ni gloria, las conciencias.[. . .]
>
> Día llegará en que un escritor valiente se decida a cortar por lo sano y a pegarle fuego a todo lo que hoy atenaza a la literatura. Será una llamarada luminosa la que se levante, entonces, sobre las bardas del corral del mundo, por encima de los adobes que cercan el garito de hospicianos del mundo. (pp. 11–14)

There is no way of knowing whether or not Cela sees himself as the one who is to make the clean break with literature that he mentions, but prologues, it must be remembered, are more than an excuse to write in italics, and the *topoi* of the "I shall not tell how" and "I don't mean to say that" are among the oldest of literary conventions. What is certain is that intrinsically Cela's novel represents a rejection of literature as plot fabrication and character maintenance. It is highly significant that the word *novela* does not appear in Cela's prologue. In its place appear the many pithy comments just quoted concerning the nature of humanity. Cela continues to acknowledge the "literary" traits of his writing for reasons having to do with his reporting of life rather than his living it through the novel. *Garito de hospicianos* is a series of unnumbered titled sketches of human beings and situations that have neither interconnection nor interdependency. The subject matter is varied and is unanimous in only its pertinency to contemporary affairs and events. Some of the sketches are poetic prose passages of an essayistic nature ("*Lluvia de estrellas*"), some are more speculatively essayistic ("*La cirugía especulativa*"), many are commentaries on news bits, column fillers or ads that have appeared in newspapers, some British and American ("*El traje de novia, la pistola y otras minucias*"). Others are more narrative in nature, at least in their dealing with people who have done something ("*Gajes de dos oficios*"). But even the latter are neither short stories, character sketches, nor notes from a novel. While one could reduce the bulk of these sketches to a few quasi-philosophic attitudes or beliefs on Cela's part, this is all they would have in common. As a whole they represent a series of often very perceptive observations on Cela's part of humanity as, according to the subtitle, a "*guirigay de imposturas y bambollas.*"

It is in this rejection of every single device reminiscent of the novel, including the word itself, and the newspaper-column observation of life that testify to *Garito de hospicia-*

nos' definitive break with Cela's previous narrative prose fiction. One reviewer has been quick to see this double circumstance of the work. Francisco Umbral writes that

> *Garito de hospicianos* no se corresponde exactamente con el último Cela — el que, para bien o para mal, tan preocupados trae a los críticos —, sino que se trata de una especie de *summa periodística* — aunque incompleta — donde el autor nos brinda su actividad como cronista voluntario y espontáneo de la vida que pasa, de la noticia real, del eterno pintoresquismo del mundo reflejado cada día en la tinta de los periódicos.[20]

If the literary but non-novelistic nature of Cela's latest work has been established to a sufficient degree, one naturally turns to a consideration of where exactly it is to be placed in the spectrum of literary typology. Fernández Molina, who spoke of *Tobogán de hambrientos* before the publication of *Garito de hospicianos*, mentioned at that time the similarity between Cela and Larra:

> Para mí, Cela siempre me ha parecido un sucesor de Larra. Tanto le duelen prendas a uno como al otro y aunque aparentemente no se parecen, su sangre de escritor es la misma. Los tiempos han cambiado, ha evolucionado la literatura y las condiciones sobre las que se desenvuelve. Es indudable que Larra no escribiría como entonces pero seguramente le preocuparían cosas muy semejantes a las que preocupan a Cela.[21]

Although this critic's reaction to *Garito de hospicianos* is not on record, it is likely that he would find his reference to Larra more than marginally borne out by the work at hand. And this is the crux of the matter in discussing the artistic development of Cela's literature: he has come to forge himself an expressive vehicle that places him, willy-nilly, precisely in the tradition of the *artículo de costumbres*.

Costumbrismo in Spain, as in other parts of Europe and Latin America, is an outgrowth of romanticism and its ironic observation of the individual in his circumstance. Although in many ways a reaction to the excesses of romantic rhetoric and the romantic sensibility, *costumbrismo* demonstrates in its awareness of the universal as it is to be attained through the particular one of the permanent and lasting contributions of the romantic revolt to modern literature. This contribution is evident in the two parallel developments of *costumbrismo* in the novel and in the essay.

It is more than merely circumstantial that the regional novel of the mid-nineteenth century often appears to us today to be a hybrid of romanticism and realism. The works of Cecilia Böhl von Faber ("*Fernán Caballero*"), Pedro Antonio de Alarcón, José María de Pereda, to mention the best-known writers of this group, are steppingstones in the development of the novel. The novel of the late nineteenth century is in one sense a restoration of the social novel of the eighteenth century developed in bourgeois France and England. The mitigating difference, however, between the novel of the eighteenth and nineteenth century is the contribution of romanticism via the *novela de costumbres.*

Despite the many novelists writing in this vein, Spain's contribution has been more in the essay. Writers such as Serafín Estébanez Calderón, Ramón de Mesonero Romanos, and Mariano José de Larra have left an extensive body of literature that demonstrates the dependency of *costumbrismo* on romantic irony while at the same time attesting to the clear-headed social criticism that is beginning to emerge at this time to replace the froth of romantic invective.

Larra is perhaps the most widely known of this group and certainly its greatest representative. Larra, typically, is to be characterized as both romantic and antiromantic. He looks back to an earlier fashion in his drama *Macías* (1834) and in the novel on the same theme, *El doncel de don Enrique el doliente* (1834). But his essays are among the most forward-looking literature of his day. Larra's *artículos de costumbres* are to be remembered for their stylistic and thematic versatility, ranging from the tongue-in-cheek spoof on Madrid society to biting satires on man and mores, which at times verge on what we today would call black humor. Employing many varying techniques, Larra's essays are noted for the way in which they depart from the essay as Montaigne conceived of it and for their frequent resemblance to short stories or novelistic essays.

The *artículo de costumbres* underwent a decline in Spain with the rise of the great novel of the last quarter of the century. It would be inaccurate to say that they disappeared completely, for a minor production has continued to survive in the nonspeculative essay of journalism and the literary reviews. It is this dormant potential that Cela has activated in his *Garito de hospicianos.*

Such a turn of events cannot, however, be taken as a sudden occurrence. Cela's latest book, if not a natural and teleological development out of his previous literature, can at least be explained in terms of what Cela has produced to date. Both Cela's novels, seen intrinsically and in terms of their prologues, and Cela's travelogues affirm and reiterate their author's painstaking attempt to approximate life and to make of his writing a human document of his time.

La familia del héroe

Were I concluding this study with comments on *Garito de hospicianos*, I should be forced to acknowledge Cela's departure, definitive for the moment, from the fold of the novelists. One extrinsic importance of the 1963 work is its sharp contrast with Cela's works that we can readily accept as novels. However, Cela has recently published *La familia del héroe, o discurso histórico de los ultimos restos (ejercicios para una sola mano)*.[22] It is a curious work, the work of a sophisticated and highly cynical observer of mankind. At the same time, Cela's recent novel adds little to our understanding of his novelistic procedure.

As a work of fiction, *La familia del héroe* demonstrates Cela's continued inspiration by the new novel, a tendency in his fiction that began with *Mrs. Caldwell habla con su hijo* and matured with *Tobogán de hambrientos.* The most prominent characteristic of Cela's work is the new novel's substitution of pattern for plot.[23] In the novel, Evangelino Gadoupa Faquitrós, grandson of the hero, don Samuel Faquitrós, relates to a group of *contertulianos* the history of his illustrious family. The novel is divided into nine sections, each one occasioned by the vermouth that don Evangelino has ordered in the preceding chapter: *Primer vermú, Segundo vermú . . . Noveno y último vermú.* Don Evangelino describes the grotesque descendants of his heroic grandfather in a monologue that forms the bulk of the text. In terms of pattern, it is significant that Cela interrupts to describe don Evangelino in *Quinto vermú,* the central segment of the work.

Cela adheres to another technique of the new novel, the eschewing of internalization and the restriction of the subject matter to phenomena and *realia* that can be observed "objectively." When one of the listeners interrupts the speaker to offer a possible explanation for the behavior of one of the latter's relatives, he is told: "Pues, mire usted, yo no le digo ni que sí ni que no: yo me limito a contarles a ustedes las cosas, tal como fueron" (p. 39). In another instance, "les estoy contando a ustedes la historia de mi familia. El conjunto de las historias de todas las familias españolas, es la historia de España, la historia de la patria de nuestros mayores. La objetividad más absoluta es el mejor adorno del historiador" (p. 70). This last statement serves also as an orientation for the novel's theme. Cela is concerned, basically, with deflating the Spanish national sense of pride, a pride he sees as ill-founded and pretentious, given the nature of man and the farce he calls life. On a higher level, Cela takes exception to the supposed dignity of man. The reader may, as an individual, take exception to Cela's vision of man and the increasing crudity of his expression.

Although acknowledging that Cela is still the most accomplished novelist and the best craftsman of the Spanish language since the Civil War, one notes that Cela's vision of mankind has failed to make any significant advances during the last five years or so and that he seems to be committed to an expressive format that allows for a certain amount of structural virtuosity, but that also has ceased to yield any new contributions to our understanding of the author's concept of the novel.

Conclusions

A BASIC premise of this study has been that Cela's novels are essentially experimental in nature. Cela's novels have often attracted more attention to their form than to their themes, and the author has stated his interest in trying out various modes of the novel.[1] It is unnecessary to discuss why Cela is interested in experimenting with different modes of fiction. Why does any author experiment with form and technique if it is not in order to find the most convenient form of self-expression? Cela's novels follow few a priori assumptions concerning the novel. In trying several different theoretical orientations, Cela has sought directly to improve his skill as a novelist and indirectly to serve as bellwether for the post-war Spanish novelists. It remains to be seen how much impression Cela's work will have on novelists in general and whether his importance will be felt sufficiently outside of Spain to influence non-Spanish novelists.

From a theoretical point of view, the principal concern of Cela's novels has been the mode of the novel as a reflection of human experience. Cela's various attempts with narrative prose fiction may be seen as seeking to establish an optimum balance between the novel and the living reality it pretends to reflect. In this respect, Cela's novels may be grouped into four broad categories: (1) traditional in form (*La familia de Pascual Duarte*); (2) novel of psychological introspection

(*Pabellón de reposo*); (3) novel of the social complex (*Nuevas andanzas y desventuras de Lazarillo de Tormes, La colmena, La catira*, and *Tobogán de hambrientos*); and (4) new novel in form (*Mrs. Caldwell habla con su hijo, Garito de hospicianos*, and *La familia del héroe. Tobogán* also shares characteristics of this group.)

Although *La familia de Pascual Duarte* is essentially traditional in form, within the broader perspective of the novelistic tendencies of Cela's maturity one can see to what extent it incorporates practices that predominate in Cela's later novels. The two most important indications are the ethical web of society and reader-distancing. The first, which reaches its most typical expression in *La colmena*, is present in the necessity the reader feels for understanding the tragedy of Duarte's existence within the total social context of his life. This necessity is suggested by the title of the novel and is reinforced by its basic irony. Although the novel is written in the first person, Cela very deftly makes his point that Duarte is incapable of understanding his plight fully. In so doing, Cela establishes the basic thematic premise of his novel that the individual is unaware of his place in life. Comments on Cela's first novel emphasize the author's concept of society as the totality of human behavior rather than any given set of national or regional institutions. This concept of society and the belief that the common man is unaware of the scope of society and his place in it form the basis of Cela's four novels that are ethical and social in orientation.

With regard to reader-distancing, Cela's desire to withdraw, leaving the reader without a convenient authority for the narrative, may be seen as an attempt to distance the reader from the narrative. The fact that the reader cannot question the details as they are presented and the fact that his faith in Duarte as a source of information is destroyed by Cela's structural irony tend to cause the reader to look upon the narrative with a skeptical eye. Unfortunately, the fundamental error in Cela's technique is that he creates distance without really intending to alienate the sympathies of the audience for

Pascual. At least, the result is a reader who is ambivalent toward Pascual. Cela's first novel is traditional, with a format that ostensibly demands reader identification and sympathy. That Cela complicates his readers' approach to the subject is indicative of a tendency that later predominates as a conscious technique.

Pabellón de reposo comes as a surprise after the violence and fast pace of *La familia de Pascual Duarte.* Nevertheless, a close examination of its pages reveals a resigned despair similar to Duarte's feelings that break through several times while he is writing his memoirs and awaiting death. Yet, what is most impressive in Cela's second novel is the almost complete renunciation of any social theme and the complete abstraction of man on an emotional level. *Pabellón de reposo* will always remain as a sort of anomaly in Cela's fiction because of the degree to which it avoids the contextual and ethical identification of its characters. At the same time, *Pabellón de reposo* has certain well-defined new-novel characteristics that are manifest in its organization and that also foreshadow Cela's later technical development, in particular the tendency to treat individuals as objects and to consider them fixed in time and history. For all of the novel's concentration upon human emotion qua individual psychology, the seven characters in their very anonymity complement one another, giving a unified impression of the anguish of man in the face of death. The same result could have been obtained through the use of one individual. The use of several with nearly identical reactions leads the reader to the assumption that he is witnessing an elemental human emotion common to all men. The belief that all men are basically and universally the same has already been shown to be fundamental to a novel like *Tobogán de hambrientos.* In addition, by choosing to fix time and history in the course of the narrative and by concentrating upon two sets of simultaneous emotions from two separate points in time rather than upon a continuum of character development, the author emphasizes both the abstract nature of his novel and its supposed universality. The assumption is, what is elemental and common to all men does not require narrative development, only exposition. In order to clarify this assumption, *Pabellón de reposo* is a contrived situation. In its contrivance and in its character anonymity/unanimity, Cela's second novel points up several theoretical considerations despite the significant lack of a social context.

The third group of novels represents the main bulk of Cela's production. Consequently, they may be taken as most typical of what Cela is trying to accomplish as a novelist. This group includes *Nuevas andanzas y desventuras de Lazarillo de Tormes*, *La colmena*, *La catira*, and *Tobogán de hambrientos*.

In Cela's third novel, the *Lazarillo*, we see utilized for the first time the ethical web of human society as the background of the novel. The analysis of this novel has taken pains to refute the common critical opinion that dismisses Cela's novel as an excellent but unimportant imitation of the earlier anonymous work. Lazarillo may be seen as the *homo viator* who is typical of man and of the emergence of his maturity through the haphazard contact with the rest of mankind that characterizes his life. In the end we know more about mankind in general, as reflected in Lazarillo's various masters, than we do about Lazarillo himself. This ending is indicative of the perspective of the novel.

Cela continues along these same lines in *La colmena*, where he is able to create a panoramic vision of society by using the perspective introduced in the *Lazarillo*. *La colmena* brings together several of Cela's earlier characteristics as a novelist and also establishes the common theoretical denominator of his fiction. *La colmena* is essentially a social or ethical novel, and the Jungian collective unconscious has been suggested as a possible philosophical source for Cela's orientation. It is here that Cela improves upon the concept of humanity as an anonymous complex of common human emotions. Seeing *La colmena* as little more than a picture of the lower-middle-class Madrid society of the years following the Civil War is just as erroneous as seeing *La familia de Pascual*

Duarte as a general indictment of Spanish society. Cela's novels go beyond the narrow limits to deal with basic human problems, an interpretation that seems evident for *Pabellón de reposo* but is complicated by the specific social contexts of the other novels. That Cela's novels have a social context is only natural in view of the fact that man is a social animal and in view of Cela's desire to examine man on the universal rather than the individual level. This latter assumption is supported by the fact that, while in *La colmena* and in the other social novels Cela goes to great pains to identify individuals, he is always careful to avoid extensive characterization and personality development. In this way, the treatment of individuals in *Pabellón de reposo* and in *La colmena* is very similar. The latter novel merely acknowledges the existence of identifiable individuals while denying that they are particularly important as individuals. The author seeks instead to fit them within a broader framework of mankind as a unified society. Critics who accuse Cela of clumsy and imperfect characterization deny any importance this procedure might have as the goal of the novel. And, too, the structural and stylistic devices that Cela employs to maintain audience-distancing lend credence to the belief that Cela intends for the reader not to identify with the characters of the novel as individuals, but to see them as forming one complex but homogeneous entity.

In view of these assumptions, it is not too surprising that Cela consented to write *La catira*. For while its focal point is the Venezuelan countryside, Cela is able to use the same novelistic practices to provide comment on man and his behavior that differs from *La colmena* only in the details of its elaboration. *La catira* follows the same Jungian tendency in the novel, carrying it a step further through the utilization of the archetypal pattern. That Cela's novel follows many of the principles of the novels of the collective unconscious in this respect is more interesting than surprising. *La catira* possesses certain stylistic characteristics that make it unique as a work of art, but these very characteristics are indicative of the author's desire for extensive reader-distancing and for an illusion of objectivity fundamental to all of Cela's novels.

Tobogán de hambrientos demonstrates to an abundant degree all of the tendencies and characteristics of Cela's novels as a whole. Cela continues to advance the idea that mankind can be seen only as a totality of individuals who share common desires, problems, and emotions. *Tobogán de hambrientos* views individuals essentially as objects to be used as raw material in a commentary upon mankind. With this novel, Cela reaches a plateau of technical achievement where successive novels threaten to become repetitions of what has already been said. Although Cela has firmly established the right of the novel to explore mankind communally from a superior point of view, it remains to be seen to what extent such a procedure can make the necessary transition from caricature to profound statements of synthesis. *Tobogán de hambrientos,* which has its obvious merits as a novel, unfortunately tends to be more caricature than profound synthesis in spite of the structural design employed in order to simulate narrative unity.

The fourth type of novel attempted by Cela is represented best by *Mrs. Caldwell habla con su hijo,* unusual in its concentration upon the individual and in its lack of any intent to project his behavior onto a universal plane. This novel is important in Cela's career for the development of techniques for reader-distancing in accord with devices for objectivity worked out by the new novel. Such devices correspond to Cela's belief in the documentary goal of the novel. Although the illusion of objectivity is sought after in Cela's previous works, *Mrs. Caldwell habla con su hijo* is the first novel to work out a series of structural devices for this purpose. Cela's satisfaction with them is evident in their incorporation into the structures of both *La catira* and *Tobogán de hambrientos.*

Tobogán de hambrientos, in particular, employs many of the devices of the new novel, especially in its use of pattern and in the rejection of chronology, definable plot, and unified points of view. Cela's *Garito de hospicianos* is an extreme example of the rejection of the more conventional narrative or fictional aspects of the novel; one could say that it would be easier to exclude it from any discussion of the novel than to attempt to justify its inclusion. I have chosen to include this work in my study if for no other reason than for the contrast that may be seen between it and Cela's earlier works and for its place in Cela's preoccupation with the novel as an appropriate vehicle for the expression of the artist's view of man. Cela's most recent novel, *La familia del héroe*, reveals the author's commitment for the time being to the new novel as the most appropriate form for his artistic expression.

Although it would be difficult to maintain that Cela's novels represent an unbroken line of development, culminating in a masterpiece that incorporates all previous works, it is possible to maintain that the novels discussed in this study represent an attempt to find a suitable form of narrative prose fiction. Cela has sought a form that will enable him, first as a man and only second as a novelist, to express what he believes to be the basic and fundamental nature of mankind and to express it in such a way that the reader will be able to stand back and see himself and his fellow man in perspective.

Cela's role as a novelist and his role as a man constitute a fundamental paradox that accounts for many of the technical and structural pecularities of his novels. Cela has come to believe that the function of the novel is to give the illusion of reflecting life as it is being lived, although, of course, the final result is but one novelist's personal vision. Cela's novels stand back to record the scurrying and the scuffle, both tragic and comic, of everyday life. In so doing he has expressed his belief that man is essentially unaware of the role he plays in the vast complex of human existence. Cela has stated both in his prologues and in his novelistic asides that the majority of men and women are unconscious of life above the level of their basest needs and desires. Cela goes a step further to affirm that reflection upon mankind's plight and any sadness thereupon are forms of atavism, although I suspect that this is Cela's way of saying that the artist is an outsider to the mainstream of life. These beliefs have been brought out particularly in *La colmena* and *Tobogán de hambrientos*, but they are valid also with reference to others of Cela's novels, for example, in the central irony of *La familia de Pascual Duarte*.

Cela's paradox lies, then, in the fact that, as a writer who is supposedly creating an imitation of life in his novel, he is forced to come to grips with the plight of mankind, to ponder it, and to shape his novelistic world accordingly. In so doing, Cela is practicing the very atavism against which he has spoken. Nevertheless, Cela has guarded himself against sadness while at the same time raising himself to a level of perception superior to that of the common man by means of the various devices for audience-distancing that have been discussed. Audience-distancing refers to two external levels of the novel: the author and the reader. It is the former about which Cela is most concerned.

Cela's first two novels constitute two rather clumsy and inexpert attempts to resolve the conflict posed by the *sine qua non* existence of the author and what he feels to be a need for objectivity. For example, in *La familia de Pascual Duarte* Cela attempts to solve the problem by giving the impression of having withdrawn entirely from his novel. The elements of mystery — the unanswered and unanswerable questions — left by the autobiographical form chosen by Cela have been discussed at length. In employing such an orientation and in making Pascual seemingly unaware of so much of what is happening to him, the novel leaves much unexplained. This procedure is essentially an error in judgment on the part of the young Cela. *Pascual Duarte*, of all of Cela's novels, has the strongest point to make, the loudest message to articulate. The failure of the novel to make a clear statement and the resulting ambiguity shown in the full spectrum of critical interpretations available to the reader have forced Cela to step in and make his point clear in writings external to the novel, never a commendable necessity. Cela's intent was to achieve a sense of objectivity by belying the ever-present filter of the author's mind and prejudices through which the content must necessarily pass in the writing. How necessary such a sense of objectivity is remains a moot question, since it detracts from rather than contributes to the structure of Cela's first novel.

On the other hand, *Pabellón de reposo* shows an author who substantiates the supposed objectivity of his narrative through the affirmation of his presence, seen in both the elaborate artifice of the novel and in the frequent interruptions of a narrator who makes no attempt to hide the fact that he is Camilo José Cela. Here the author feels it necessary to insist that the patients whose writings he utilizes are nothing but figments of his imagination. Cela does this facetiously to allay the fear that he is portraying individuals so true to life that they will have a bad effect on real patients—facetiously because Cela means them just to be so, that is, true to life—and also in order to promote the process of emotional abstraction underlying the novel. In so doing, Cela establishes the documentary nature of his novel and sets himself up as a superior point of intelligence for the human situation. This is, after all, what every author has done since men began narrating. Any sense of objectivity derives from the fashion in which the author approaches human experience, through a few simultaneous realities of the moment, and from the degree to which he prevents the reader from entering the cosmos of the novel and identifying with any of its characters.

In both *Nuevas andanzas y desventuras de Lazarillo de Tormes* and *Mrs. Caldwell habla con su hijo*, Cela side-steps the issue of objectivity completely by attributing the physical substance of the narrative to unapproachable sources, albeit sources that are more plausible and better worked out than that of Pascual Duarte's memoirs.

Since both Lázaro and Mrs. Caldwell are likely sources for their papers, no problem of objectivity is created. In Lázaro's narrative, Lázaro, as the alter ego of Cela, serves to put forth Cela's belief in society as human interaction. In being present as the internal observer in the person of Lázaro, Cela is able directly to establish his intent for the novel in a way much more subtle than in his two previous novels. Mrs. Caldwell, on the other hand, may have been more or less unaware of her mental deterioration. However, that unawareness is not the point of the novel. It is rather one of a simple documentation of her insanity and a question of any relation the reader might see between the behavior of the insane Mrs. Caldwell and the majority of so-called sane men. The position of the author is, therefore, of no particular importance. The position of the reader, on the other hand, is of primary importance.

In *La colmena* Cela is able to withdraw as the narrator, and for the first time the reader has before him the novel as a human document that the author has sought to create. *La colmena* has no narrator who functions on the level of the narrative, as is the case in Cela's earlier novels. Nevertheless, the reader is constantly aware of the presence of a guiding hand that not only edits the world of the novel but also arranges its portrayal in the most artificial of ways in order to make its point. *La colmena* is an unretouched picture of life, but seen through the most overt of lenses. Although the author attempts to remain above the level of his narrative in order to create an illusion of objectivity, it is safe to say that it is an objectivity that derives more from the technical devices of the author for avoiding subjectivity on both his part and that of the reader rather than from any real objectivity.

The same is basically true of *La catira*. There is a narrator whose language identifies him more closely with the narrative than with the reader. Yet, the technical devices of the novel are such that the reader is sufficiently distanced, and the conscious narrator does not participate in the unconscious mythic elements of the narrative. Thus, we may speak of a lack of involvement on the part of both narrator and reader.

Tobogán de hambrientos, *Garito de hospicianos*, and *La familia del héroe* also are related by narrators who speak on the level of their characters. However, Cela's recent works affirm explicitly what *La catira* implies: that a narrator who is aware of what he is describing cannot be a part of what he narrates. This is the idea of the unconscious masses who act out their grim and absurd part unself-consciously and without regret.

It is significant that Cela's recent novels represent in many aspects the culmination of his desire for a sense of objectivity on the part of both author and reader. Cela has dropped the pretense of not being present in his work and has accepted his right as an intellectual to reflect upon man's existence and to portray it as he sees fit. What is unique in his practice, at least as far as the contemporary Spanish novel is concerned, is that he is able to do this while at the same time projecting neither himself nor his audience into the narrative. Cela's attitude toward man is sardonic and superior, and he asks his reader to share his cynicism. Whether or not Cela as a man is "human" pales in the face of his rigorous design for portraying the foibles of the human race. In the process his characters become little more than tokens in an elaborately detailed exposition. The validity of their portrayal is measurable externally on the basis of the reader's own experiences. It would appear that it is on this assumption that Cela has dispensed with the traditional artifice of the novel, installed himself as a detached expert of human behavior, and distanced both himself and the reader to better enjoy the view. In this regard, what has been said concerning Bertolt Brecht and his theater is equally applicable to Cela:

> How the *Verfremdungseffekt* is to be achieved by the author Brecht discusses in his essay *Die Strassenszene*, the gist of which is that the actor's [narrator's] business is not very different from that of an eye-witness of a traffic accident who demonstrates to a quickly gathering crowd how the accident, of which he was the sole witness, occurred. With Brecht, the anti-Stanislavskij *par excellence*, the actor has become, then, a teacher with a pointer, a *philologus in actu;* he "is" not King Lear, but he "demonstrates" King Lear.[2]

Any discussion of Cela's novel is bound to be haunted by the specter not only of what the novel is as a genre but also of what a novel should consist. This study has focused on

Cela's repeated assertion that he considers a novel to be a source of information concerning mankind. In believing that men are basically the same and in writing novels that utilize typical and archetypal human personalities, Cela is basically neoclassic as a philosopher and as a theoretician on the content of art. That the novel must portray what is typical about man and mankind rather than what is singular and particular has hopefully been established as a working premise for Cela as a novelist.

Yet, the structure of Cela's novels is as far removed from traditional or classic forms as is possible. Structurally and formally speaking, Cela's novels are free forms. In a sense they are singular in their very rejection of any a priori assumptions concerning the novel in the same way that Cela's characters refuse to behave in accordance with any preconceived moral or ethical notions. This is not to say that Cela's novels lack form any more than free forms lack form. They merely adjust themselves conveniently to the stresses of the situation at hand.

Basically, however, the principal condemnation of Cela as a novelist results not from his radical designs for the novel, but from his departure from the romantic-realist pattern in which the novelist is responsible for the creation of individuals who, although they may reflect the broader outlines of their society, must also exist as well-defined and unique individuals. It is the latter that Cela refuses to have his characters do. The characters of Cela's novels gather any importance they may possess as individuals solely from their identity with the larger human society to which they belong. Since Cela seems to feel that it is unnecessary to create individuals – perhaps even impossible – he can with little trouble reject the form, devices, and ends of the realist novel. A significant step toward understanding Cela's work as a novelist is made by the reader who is able to allow himself to accept for the moment the possibility and the desirability of the novelist's speaking purely on the level of human universals. The fact that those universals may be the basest – as opposed to the lofty virtues usually associated with the classic perspective in literature—is certainly of a secondary consideration.

Only time will tell the permanent worth of Cela as a novelist and of the extent to which he has shaped the direction to be taken by the novel in Spain. Whatever the durability of Cela's work may be, attention must be paid it at this time by any literary critic or historian who is interested in understanding both the problems of the novel as a continually re-adapting form of artistic and human expression and the importance that genre in turn has come to have in the literature of contemporary Spain.

NOTES

Notes to the Introduction

1. José María Castellet, "La joven novela española," *Sur*, No. 284, 48. Although I can agree with Castellet's statements as a whole, I am at a loss to understand his next sentence, which concludes the paragraph: "Los autores más conocidos son Camilo José Cela y Miguel Delibes." This study undertakes to show the untenability of listing Cela as traditional in his approach to the novel.

2. Sherman Eoff's *Modern Spanish Novel* is, in part, futile because of this rejection of naturalism. His examination of the modern Spanish novel through a comparison of selected Spanish works with non-Spanish "prototypes" leads inevitably to the conclusion that the Spanish novel relied on imitation and that it never quite matched the supposed model in technical accomplishment. Of course, the question arises as to whether or not the Spanish novel did indeed attempt to imitate foreign models. Eoff does not discuss this point, and one concludes that he is trying to show that the modern Spanish novel shares the same tendencies as the non-Spanish. It may, but Eoff's study makes it obvious that the Spaniards contributed little or nothing to those tendencies. All in all, Eoff's analyses of the individual works are excellent and revealing, showing that, if nothing else, the modern Spanish novel has not been so bad or so unimaginative as has been claimed.

3. My remarks on realism are based on the essay by René Wellek, "The Concept of Realism in Literary Scholarship," in his *Concepts of Criticism*, 222–55.

4. For a discussion of the major developments in the contemporary novel, see Walter Allen, *The Modern Novel in Britain and the United States*; Mariano Goyanes Baquero, *Proceso de la novela actual*; William Van O'Connor, *Forms of Modern Fiction*. With reference to the importance of the developments in character portrayal, see W. J. Harvey, *Character and the Novel*, and Charles I. Glicksberg, *The Self in Modern Literature*.

5. Robert Humphrey, *Stream of Consciousness in the Modern Novel*, 2. See also Leon Edel, *The Modern Psychological Novel*. For a recent study that explores in depth an aspect of the novel tangential to stream of consciousness, see Bertil Romberg, *Studies in the Narrative Technique of the First-Person Novel*.

6. See A. A. Mendilow, *Time and the Novel*; Hans Meyerhoff, *Time in Literature*; and Margaret Church, *Time and Reality*.

7. See Edwin Moseley's useful study, *Pseudonyms of Christ in the Modern Novel*. Moseley discusses the use of one such mythic archetype in contemporary fiction.

8. See Davis Dunbar McElroy, *Existentialism and Modern Literature*.

9. For an example of how such literature elaborates a tragic vision of man, see Charles I. Glicksberg, *The Tragic Vision in Twentieth-Century Literature*.

10. Castellet, "La joven novela española," 50–51.

11. See the discussions of this subject in Sergio Pacifici, *A Guide to Contemporary Italian Literature*.

12. See Alain Robbe-Grillet, *Pour un nouveau roman*, and Laurent Le Sage, *The French New Novel*.

13. See José Vilá Selam, *Tres ensayos sobre la literatura y nuestra guerra*.

14. Domingo Pérez Minik, *Novelistas españoles de los siglos XIX, XX*, 259–60.

15. See José Sánchez, "Los premios literarios españoles," *Kentucky Foreign Language Quarterly*, 6 (1959), 189–94. Sánchez counts 175.

16. William J. Grupp, "Contemporary Spanish Literary and Intellectual Life," *Modern Language Journal*, 45 (April, 1961), 158, 159. See also Edmund Stephen Urbanski, "El revisionismo en la valoración de las letras y cultura contemporánea de España," *Hispania*, 48 (December, 1965), 816–25.

17. A relatively complete list of criticism dealing with Cela is to be found in the commemorative issue devoted to Cela: "Camilo José Cela: Bibliografía," *Revista hispánica moderna*, 28 (April–October, 1962), 210–20. See also the Bibliography at the end of this study.

18. Olga Prjevalinsky, *El sistema estético de Camilo José Cela, expresividad y estructura*; Paul Ilie, *La novelística de Camilo José Cela*; Alonso Zamora Vicente, *Camilo José Cela acercamiento a un escritor*; Robert Kirsner, *The Novels and Travels of Camilo José Cela*. In terms of usefulness, I would rank them: Prjevalinsky, Ilie, Zamora Vicente, Kirsner. Reference is made to these works, in part or in whole, at appropriate places in the study.

19. D. L. Shaw, "[Review of Alonso Zamora Vicente's *Camilo José Cela*]," *Bulletin of Hispanic Studies*, 40 (1963), 257–58.

20. Basic discussions of these developments appear in: John Crowe Ransom, *The New Criticism*; Lewis Leary, *Contemporary Literary Scholarship: A Critical Review*; James E. Miller, Jr., *Myth and Method: Modern Theories of Criticism*; Wellek, "American Literary Scholarship" and "The Main Trends of Twentieth-Century Criticism," in *Concepts of Criticism*, 296–315 and 344–64, respectively; and Wayne C. Booth, *Rhetoric of Fiction*.

21. See Richard Chase, *The Quest for Myth*. A chapter of this book is reprinted in the Miller collection cited in the preceding note. One of the new critics whose theoretical approach attempts to seek out the archetypal patterns of literature, in a sort of synthesis of form and mythic archetype, is Northrup Frye; see his *Anatomy of Criticism*.

Notes to Chapter 1

1. First published in Barcelona, Destino, 1942. Our text is the fourteenth edition (Barcelona, Destino, 1963).

2. Apropos to this procedure, Nathalie Sarraute, in her *L'ère du soupçon*,

59–60, has attributed it to a demand originating with the reader: "Et tout d'abord, aujourd'hui, se méfie de ce que lui propose l'imagination de l'auteur. 'Plus personne, se plaint M. Jacques Tournier, n'ose avouer qu'il invente. Le documente seul importe, précis, daté, vérifié, authentique. L'oeuvre d'imagination est bannie, parce qu'inventée . . . [Le public] a besoin, pour croire à ce qu'on lui raconte, d'être sûr qu'on ne le "lui fait pas." . . . Plus rien ne compte que le petit fait vrai' . . ."

3. At the risk of simplifying a complex phenomenon, we might say that it is an objectivity born of an insecurity in the face of reality as we perceive it. Once man has been intimidated by reality into fearing that it is not as he seems to experience it, all semblance of the secure omniscience of a Dickens must crumble. For an excellent analysis of this progressive insecurity and its effects upon the novel, see Eoff, *The Modern Spanish Novel.*

4. Sherman Eoff, "Tragedy of the Unwanted Person in Three Versions: Pablo de Segovia, Pito Pérez, Pascual Duarte," *Hispania*, 39 (May, 1956), 195. "[Pascual Duarte] represents the twentieth-century obsession with the subject of man's cosmic relevancy — or irrelevancy."

5. Zamora Vicente, *Camilo José Cela*, "La familia de Pascual Duarte," 23–50. He observes, "[el personaje de la novela es] el odio, creciente, en torrente sonoro y frío de la altura, cegador y, sin embargo, clarividente. El odio del hijo no comprendido ni acariciado jamás, el hijo que no alcanza ni siquiera una curiosidad amable por parte de su madre, verdadera biología simplicísima, sin más. El gran logro de la narración primeriza de Camilo José Cela está en esa sabia dosificatión de la vitalidad de un sentimiento, gastado en la literatura, teatralmente manejado por lo general, pero hecho aquí criatura de carne y hueso; nada de pasión espectral, sino alarmante sístole, con sus rugidos y sus silencios, que alcanza prodigiosa manifestación de cumbre al final" (p. 29). Perhaps Zamora Vicente has a point here. Paul Ilie, in his *La novelística de Camilo José Cela*, has devoted a section of his study on *Pascual Duarte* to "La estética de la violencia," (pp. 56–76). This is part of the supposed *tremendista* impact of Cela's novel. See Joseph G. Corriols, "An Analysis of 'Tremendismo' in the Novels of Camilo José Cela," and, in general, Olga Prjevalinsky Ferrer, "La literatura española y su nexo con el existencialismo," *Revista hispańica moderna*, 22 (July–October, 1956), 297–303.

6. "More than mere symbols — an interesting case might be made for Pascual Duarte's being an allegory of Spain — the literary persons are totally integrated with their habitat. However «universal» they may be, . . . they are singularly Hispanic in their structure. Only in the *particular* realm of that which is Spain can we understand the actions and motivations of all characters in *Pascual Duarte.*" Kirsner, *The Novels and Travels of Camilo José Cela*, 26. Although this work serves as an adequate introduction to Cela's "viajes," the treatment of the novels is inadequate for our orientation, inasmuch as Kirsner is less interested in the novels as autonomous works of art than he is in destroying the boundaries between art and sociology in order to discuss the characters of the novel as keys to understanding Spanish culture and related subjects.

7. Camilo José Cela, "Palabras ocasionales," in *La familia de Pascual Duarte*, edited by Harold L. Boudreau and John W. Kronik, x.

8. Camilo José Cela, "Pascual Duarte, de limpio," *Papeles de Son Armadans*, 21 (June, 1961), 227–31. Also published as the author's preface to the edition cited in this study. This essay indicates Cela's desire to clear away the fog left by the many things written about his novel and explains

his readiness to be so explicit in his words accompanying the American edition, published about the same time as this essay.

9. David M. Feldman, "Camilo José Cela and 'La familia de Pascual Duarte'," *Hispania*, 44 (December, 1961), 656–59. "Cela insists that man must be struck by the awesome fact of his complete responsibility for what he is, thinks and does. Only in such awareness can he avoid destruction. Yet precisely in this regard is Cela's optimism to be noted. He believes that man, once aware of his responsibility, is capable of its fulfillment" (p. 658).

10. Mary Ann Beck, "Nuevo encuentro con «La familia de Pascual Duarte»," *Revista hispánica moderna*, 30 (July–October, 1964), 284.

11. When Pascual is released from prison after having served three years for the death of *El Estirao*, he does go on at length about society's mistake in setting him free: "Y creyendo que me hacían un favor me hundieron para siempre" (p. 150). However, seen in the larger context of Pascual's condemnation of his own behavior, we realize that he is not accusing society for his behavior, but is lamenting its foolishness in turning loose upon itself a proven misfit who can only go further each time in his acts of violence and sudden temper until he again commits murder. This indeed proves to be true. Pascual says of himself just a few lines before these: "[. . .]y yo – este pobre yo, este desgraciado derrotado que tan poca compasión en usted y en la sociedad es capaz de provocar – [. . .]" (p. 149). This seems to be further evidence of Cela's jarring irony.

12. Zamora Vicente, *Camilo José Cela*, 39–44, "'. . . al irlo a rematar . . . , sonreía'". See p. 44 in particular. But then he also calls *El Estirao*'s death "suicide" (p. 27).

13. Paul Ilie, in *La novelística*, has already mentioned this "conflict of interests": "[Pascual Duarte] aparece demasiado consciente de sí mismo, demasiado autoanalítico, lo que significa que el escritor es consciente y analítico, pero no puede revelar su presencia. Así, la verosimilitud del carácter de Pascual resulta menoscabada cuando asume ostensiblemente funciones del autor" (p. 39).

14. The present study does not attempt to examine in detail the themes of Cela's novels; therefore, content is discussed only in so far as it is related to form. For a study of Cela's concept of man, including the original-sin motif, see R. L. Predmore, "La imagen del hombre en las obras de Camilo José Cela," *La torre*, 9 (January-March, 1961), 81–102.

Notes to Chapter 2

1. Our text is the third Spanish edition (Barcelona, Destino, 1957).

2. Ilie, *La novelística*, 77–111. Ilie's chapter is perhaps the most complete analysis to date. Unfortunately, after presenting some fine insights into the work as fiction, Ilie succumbs to the temptation to compare it with Thomas Mann's *Der Zauberberg* (pp. 94–98). The similarities are slight, and the justification that they are slight because Cela's work results from a very personal experience makes one question the value of mentioning Mann at all. Ilie's final conclusion is that *Pabellón de reposo*, while raising basic problems of existence, isolation, and death, is not a particularly significant work.

3. For general considerations, see Zamora Vicente, *Camilo José Cela*, "Novela de la inacción," 81–85: "Y, evidentemente, responde a una preoccupación que podríamos llamar *literaria*, es decir, al afán de hacer novelable el confuso y atormentado mundo silencioso de los enfermos. Al fin y al cabo,

una forma nobilísima de escapar la insidosa asechanza de la enfermedad, que exige una atención sin descanso ni interrupciones" (p. 82).

4. J. M. Castellet, "Iniciación a la obra narrativa de Camilo José Cela," *Revista hispánica moderna*, 28 (April-October, 1962), 146.

5. That is, discounting Robert Kirsner's somewhat ambiguous statements in *The Novels and Travels*: "*Pabellón de reposo* is, in effect, the placid, poetic vision of *La familia de Pascual Duarte*. It is, in other words, the first novel elevated to the realm of calm poetry. We still have the interplay of life and death, one giving meaning to the other, but it is presented in a style that is deliberately piercing. Yet, the more sensitive the mode of expression, the greater the horror. The theme and its treatment do not seem to converge; there is a lack of inherent harmony" (p. 36). Unless I am gravely in error, my conclusion is that Kirsner would see both novels treating of the same indiscriminate cruelty that is a reality of life. I would agree with this, but as a basic orientation of Cela's rather than as a concrete detail of style and theme.

6. To my knowledge, J. M. Castellet, in *Iniciación a la obra narrativa de Camilo José Cela*, is the only critic who has discussed Cela's fiction in terms of two groups: "Las novelas de intención realista o de la objetividad" (*La familia de Pascual Duarte, Nuevas andanzas y desventuras de Lazarillo de Tormes, La colmena*, and *La catira*) and "Las novelas de intención lírica o de la subjetividad" (*Pabellón de reposo* and *Mrs. Caldwell habla con su hijo*). We may add *Tobogán de hambrientos* and *La familia del héroe* to the first group.

7. To a certain extent, I am repeating things already recorded by Ilie in *La novelística*, "División formal de la novela," 77–83. Since his comments are more by way of defining the novel than of attempting to discuss it as *novel*, in the abstract sense of the word, the overlapping seems to be justified as well as necessary for completeness.

8. Olga Prjevalinsky Ferrer, *El sistema estético de Camilo José Cela*.

9. This has been the main criticism of Juan Luis Alborg, *Hora actual de la novela española* [*1ª serie*], 79–113.

10. Guillermo de Torre, "La estética de Cela aclarada por la de Solana," *Revista hispánica moderna*, 28 (April–October, 1962), 157. The reference is to Cela's paper on Solana, read on the occasion of Cela's installation in the Real Academia Española, "La obra literaria del pintor Solana." The paper has subsequently been published in Cela's *Cuatro figuras del 98*. It is worth noting what Cela has to say about *Pabellón de reposo* in his Preface: "Novela escrita con una preocupación estética, más que estilística, que por ahora no he continuado, por lo menos en el libro, sus páginas pienso que pueden ser sintomáticas e incluso clave para quienes me honran siguiendo, con cierta atención, mi labor" (p. 11).

11. See Kirsner's comments on this theme in *The Novels and Travels*, 40–42. The structure of *Pabellón de reposo* implies a division of the world into "the Healthy" and "the Sick" (see statements on pages 25, 30, 66, 73, 175, 200, and others). Since the explicit references come from the patients themselves — the author merely suggests the contrast in parts of the *Intermedio* — one may speak of it as a cosmic distinction that exists only for them. Given the references by others to the emotional instability of the patients (see statements on pages 96, 114, 115, 166, 168), thematic considerations must take into account a further dichotomy implied by the novel between reality and how it is presented through the eyes of the "outsiders" (who are, incidentally, the Enemy, the Healthy), and hallucination and fantasy as seen in the writings of the patients. The novel provides various points of

reference to aid in measuring this dichotomy: the author, the staff of the sanitarium, and the contradictions and confusions the reader is able to detect in the writings themselves.

12. The two best sources for Cela's biography are Zamora Vicente, *Camilo José Cela*, 9–20, and Camilo José Cela, "Relativo curriculum vitae," *Revista hispánica moderna*, 28 (April–October, 1962), 179–275.

13. For a discussion of the "novel within the novel," see Leon Livingstone, "Interior Duplication and the Problem of Form in the Modern Spanish Novel," *PMLA*, 73 (September, 1958), 393–406, which provides a background to the problem as well as offering some very good insights. However, it would be necessary to add to the pivotal remark, "All of these techniques constitute a conscious pursuit of total vision for the achievement of which the artist must seek to examine reality from as many points of view as possible" (p. 404), an understanding of the conflict between author and fiction as it exists in *Pabellón de reposo*. For Cela in this novel, being is only what is seen at a given moment, a belief that may or may not bring with it the necessity for more points of view, more moments, and, thus, more reality.

14. *Pabellón de reposo* (Barcelona, Destino, 1952), 11–13. Reprinted in the third edition.

15. Published originally as Camilo José Cela, "La experiencia personal en «Pabellón de reposo»," *Papeles de Son Armadans*, 24 (February, 1962), 131–35.

16. Cela, "La experiencia personal": "Esta novela es el inmediato producto de una amarga y aleccionadora experiencia personal; no me explico cómo algo tan evidente pudo dar pábulo al rumor, actitud que requiere, al menos, de un cierto velo de misterio cayendo sobre las cosas" (p. 131).

17. I am taking exception to Kirsner's analysis in *The Novels and Travels*, 42–46. One of the most serious defects of his study is a necessity he appears to feel to prove that all of Cela's works reflect the reality of Spain, a necessity that forces him to make some highly questionable statements concerning *Mrs. Caldwell habla con su hijo*, set in England, and *La catira*, set in Venezuela. In the introductory statement, Kirsner observes, "Throughout his novels the consciousness of Spain is a motivating force in his creative process . . . and this study will devote itself primarily to the consideration of the role of Spain in the novels of Cela, *i.e.*, Spain as a literary theme" (p. 16).

Notes to Chapter 3

1. Our text is the sixth Spanish edition (Barcelona, Noguer, 1955). For a selection of the press reviews and critical commentary on *Lazarillo*, see the Bibliography at the end of this study.

2. For the most complete list of Cela's publications, see "Camilo José Cela: Bibliografía," in "Relativo curriculum vitae," 210–20, and "Ediciones," 210–16. Not so complete is the list of studies, "Estudios," 216–20.

3. See Kirsner's comments in *The Novels and Travels:* "However, the characters' inner lives are not immured in antithetical emblems. Their actions are not confined to allegorical contrasts. In their freedom from disproportionate symbols, they follow an irregular pattern which does not rest on logical concepts but rather on their own personal possibilities, in varying degree logical and illogical but always singularly their own" (p. 50). "[Lazarillo's] own life is contained in the experiences of different characters. By virtue of being an active receptacle, he has a serpentine existence" (p. 51).

4. A few examples are called for here. The anonymous *Lazarillo de Tormes* draws to a close with Lázaro's changed situation in life; *La vida del Buscón* ends with Pablo's embarcation for the New World. In the contemporary Spanish novel, two examples of this technique come to mind: Carmen Laforet's *Nada* (1945), which ends with the heroine's transfer to Madrid, thus terminating her brief and unpleasant, but revealing, stay in Barcelona; and Miguel Delibes' *El camino* (1950), which leads up, by way of flashbacks, to Daniel, *el Mochuelo*'s farewell to his village as he goes away to school in Madrid. The American novel seems to find particularly inviting the theme of the teen-ager's summer vacation; during its boring months the awakening takes place, and its end brings the narrative to a necessary conclusion. The classic example is Carson McCullers' *The Member of the Wedding* (1946). Another classic example, more typical and more picaresque in its elements, is Mark Twain's perennial favorite, *Huckleberry Finn* (1884).

5. Marguerite C. Rand, "Lazarillo de Tormes, Classic and Contemporary," *Hispania*, 44 (May, 1961), 223, 228.

6. Rand, "Lazarillo de Tormes": "His Lazarillo, this modern child prodigy, does not fail to see sordid details, but with indomitable optimism he strives to enhance reality, to infuse into it some of his own vitality, in order to make his life more bearable. Reality becomes for him a fiction of the external world about him with the fantasies of his subconscious and the absurdities of his dreams. Fact and fantasy blend into a kind of superreality" (p. 225).

7. Ilie, in *La novelística*, devotes most of his chapter on the *Lazarillo* to a discussion of the novel as a key to understanding the travelogs.

8. Cela himself states in "Notas sobre la herramienta literaria," *Papeles de Son Armadans*, 14 (March, 1962), 243–46, that "Con estas «Nuevas andanzas y desventuras de Lazarillo de Tormes» quise ensayar mi madurez en el oficio de escritor" (p. 243). He concludes that "El «Lazarillo», considerado en el conjunto de mi producción literaria, es un libro crítico — valga el término clínico —, un libro que señala una época de crisis. De ella tanto pude haber salido robustecido como depauperado. Entendí necesario probar mis artes de zahorí en el bosquecillo umbrío de los clásicos, tan rico en caudalosos veneros de saludable agua clara, y abrí mi pozo al pie del árbol de Lázaro, viejo y buen amigo" (p. 246).

9. J. M. Castellet, "Iniciación a la obra narrativa," 129.

10. Kirsner, *The Novels and Travels*, 52.

11. Zamora Vicente, *Camilo José Cela*, "La vuelta al mito," 78–79.

12. Alborg, *Hora actual de la novela española*, "Camilo Jose Cela," 89. Jacqueline Praag-Chantraine, in "Chronique des lettres espagnoles: actualité du roman picaresque," *Synthèses*, 14 (May, 1959), 121–33, is concerned with the lack of traditional picaresque elements in Cela's novel, such as dramatic progression, climaxes, surprises, etc. (see p. 125 in particular), and calls it a "pastiche" (p. 125). However, Miss Praag-Chantraine's comments are obscured by the inclusion of *Pascual Duarte* and *La colmena* within the scope of her article, two works that can in no formal sense of the word be called picaresque.

Notes to Chapter 4

1. Our text is the fourth Spanish edition (Barcelona, Noguer, 1962). *La colmena* is supposedly the first title in the series, "Caminos inciertos." A

second title remains yet to be published. See the Bibliography at the end of this study for a selection of the press reviews.

2. Ilie, *La novelística*, "Consideraciones formales," 122–31.

3. See David W. Foster, "*La colmena* de Camilo José Cela y los escritos de éste sobre la novela," *Hispanófila* (to be published).

4. See John Flasher, "Aspects of Novelistic Technique in Cela's *La colmena*," *West Virginia University Philological Papers*, 21 (November, 1959), 30–43. Like Manual Durán's article, "La estructura de *La colmena*," *Hispania*, 43 (March, 1960), 19–24, Flasher's paper is rather sketchy in its approach. Neither attempts to survey the structural design of Cela's work or to arrive at any conclusions as to Cela's concept of the novel.

5. Cela does not number the various briefer narrative units that make up his novel. Chapter I has 47; II, 45; III, 25; IV, 41; V, 28; VI, 9; "Final," 18. This study refers to them as follows: (I.17, 40), *i.e.*, Chapter I, narrative unit 17, beginning on p. 40 of the fourth Spanish edition.

6. Flasher's article provides sketches of the most outstanding of these personalities, as well as others in the novel.

7. Gonzalo Torrente Ballester, *Panorama de la literatura española contemporánea*, 449.

8. Flasher, "Aspects of Novelistic Technique," 31.

9. With respect to Cela's identification with his characters, see Ilie's remark in *La novelística* that "no sugiero necesariamente que Cela sea exacto en su pintura, sino que es sensitivo al grupo sin hallarse especialmente orientado hacia él" (p. 135).

10. Reproduced in our edition, p. 15.

11. Although bibliographic information is not available for *La colmena*, Miss Theile-Bruhns' name is associated with other translations of Cela into German, and thus her existence is "authenticated." See *Mrs. Caldwell spricht mit ihrem Sohn*, aus dem Spanischen von Gerda Theile-Bruhns (Zurich, Verlag der Arche, 1961).

12. See Ilie, *La novelística*, "El tiempo," 126–29.

13. For a discussion of *La colmena* as a "behaviorist" novel, see Gustavo Martínez Bueno, "*La colmena*, novela behaviorista," *Clavileño*, 3 (September-October, 1952), 53–58. Concerning what he means by "behaviorism," Martínez Bueno writes: "que todos los misterios de la vida, singularmente de la vida psíquica, deben ser formulados según el esquema *estímulo-reacción*. Considérese esta tesis, que niega la vida interior, como una renunciación provisional a abarcar toda la realidad vital en aras de un mayor rigor en los resultados. [. . .]*La colmena* constituye [. . .]el modelo consumado de la aplicación de la actitud behaviorista" (p. 56). This thesis unfortunately fails to take into account the numerous times Cela reports interior monologue or thoughts. Also, behaviorist psychology usually does not admit the superior and omnisicient point of view that Cela accepts as his birthright, so to speak, as a novelist. Nevertheless, Martínez's observations support my premise concerning the basic perspective of the novel as a form of fiction.

14. To avoid confusion, it must be understood that it is the author who is speaking in this paragraph.

15. Concerning the role of Martín Marco, see José Ortega, "Importancia del personaje Martín Marco en *La colmena* de Cela," *Romance Notes*, 7 (Spring, 1965), 92–95. He writes: "Se ha dicho que *La colmena* [. . .] carece de personaje central y también se ha afirmado que Martín, una de las figuras de esta novela, no es más que un instrumento técnico para polarizar acciones. El siguiente comentario tratará de probar que Martín Marco debe

ser considerado como el protagonista central de *La colmena* por ser el que de una forma más clara y completa ejemplifica los problemas de orden ético del autor" (p. 92).

Notes to Chapter 5

1. Our text is the second Spanish edition (Barcelona, Destino, 1958). See the Bibliography at the end of this study for a selection of the press reviews. No critical study to date deals specifically with this novel.

2. Camilo José Cela, *Viaje a la Alcarria* (Madrid, Revista de Occidente, 1948).

3. See Ilie, *La novelística*, "Mrs. Caldwell habla con su hijo," 150–208. See in particular "Madre a hijo," 165–85.

4. Kirsner, in *The Novels and Travels*, speaks also of the "Freudian symbols" of the narrative (p. 86). Kirsner's near cry of defeat in the face of interpreting the novel gives the reader a fair idea of the usual critical reaction: "In the last analysis, the reality of the book will reflect the readers' experiences. This novel, more than any other of Cela, demands participation on the part of the audience. Completeness would destroy it. Thus, the novel will take the form of the personal moment" (p. 85). This observation has not prevented Kirsner from advancing his own personal interpretation that *Mrs. Caldwell* is an allegory of Spain speaking to her sons lost in the Civil War (p. 86). This interpretation seems largely fanciful, especially because Kirsner offers no support, textual or otherwise, for such an assumption.

5. This paucity of plot has led Zamora Vicente to admit that *Mrs. Caldwell* is a bore. In his *Camilo José Cela*, "Evocando sueños," 85–87, he writes: "Decididamente, es un descanso volver la última página y saber que Mrs. Caldwell está, para morir, en un hospital de lunáticos. A pesar del cuidadoso laborar de Camilo José Cela por obtener un libro lleno de nieblas oníricas, a pesar, reconozcámoslo, de sus aciertos expresivos y de su tino en el desarrollo del libro, digamos también que nos encontramos mucho más a gusto cuando el autor nos lleva de la mano, paisaje cambiante y luminoso, por una carretera de España adentro [, como lo hace en sus libros de viajes]" (p. 87). With regard to the dream aspect of *Mrs. Caldwell*, see Ilie, *La novelística*, "Surrealismo," 198–208.

6. See Laurent Le Sage, *The French New Novel: An Introduction and a Sampler*. The following remarks rely upon Le Sage's excellent introduction and documentation.

7. These two characteristics are observed in the various terms employed by critics with reference to this new type of novel: *roman blanc* (Bernard Dort, writing of Robbe-Grillet, Jean Cayrol, and Paul Gadenne), *anti roman* (Alain Bosquet, of Maurice Blanchot; from Sartre, of Nathalie Sarraute), *roman experimental* (Gaëton Picon, of Michel Butor), *ante roman* (Bernard Pingaud), *jeune roman* (Maurice Nadeau, of Samuel Beckett, Kateb Yacine, and Jacques Cousseau). *Nouveau roman* seems to have been established as the generic term by *Ésprit*, the Paris review that in 1958 published a report on the new novel and a list of its representatives. See Le Sage, *The French New Novel*, 3, 42–44.

8. Le Sage summarizes: "The new novel, limiting itself to recording the reactions of a consciousness without any conceptual assumptions whatever follows so exactly the philosophical method advocated by Edmund Husserl and popularized in France by Sartre that the word phenomenology seems

the only one which will do. The complex question of psychology and the new novel resolves itself in this — psychology has been replaced by phenomenology" (p. 16). The point-of-view technique is used effectively by Cela in *Pabellón de reposo* and *La colmena,* although in the latter novel analytic technique vies for predominance with point-of-view. However, Cela is never guilty of being the heavy-handed moral and ethical authoritarian that his predecessors in analysis are. Cela never helps us out in our evaluation by making an overt judgment, but simply provides additional information. In *Mrs. Caldwell,* Cela allows the woman to speak for herself.

9. Le Sage, *The French New Novel,* 17.

10. Le Sage, *The French New Novel,* 32.

11. There is one other technical aspect of the French new novel that does not apply to Mrs. Caldwell. Le Sage concludes his comments on dialogue in *The French New Novel* by saying that it "has an important place in the new novel, but is not the sort usually encountered. These writers do not bring their characters together periodically to advance the story and create lifelike atmosphere by having them discourse. Conversation occurs as something floating on the surface of consciousness, trivial or inoffensive in appearance but indicative of mysterious activity beneath" (p. 39).

12. Ilie, *La novelística,* 151.

13. Sarraute, *L'ère du soupçon,* 70–71. Quoted in English by Le Sage, p. 14.

14. The reader is also referred to the "Algunas palabras al que leyere." In this introduction, written in July, 1952, the follower of Cela's career will find Cela's first analysis of his techniques: "Esta *Mrs. Caldwell* es la quinta novela que publico y la quinta *técnica de novelar* — ¡qué horrorosa y pedantesca expresión! — que empleo" (p. 10). Cela discusses each of his first four novels in terms of the novelistic technique it demonstrates (he prefers not to discuss his fifth novel for its recency) and thus calls the first round in the polemic as to whether or not his several novels indeed represent an equal number of diverse techniques. Needless to say, the present study is responding to the need for an extensive discussion of this subject.

15. See Oscar Büdel, "Contemporary Theater and Aesthetic Distance," *PMLA,* 76 (June, 1961), 277–91: "All Brecht achieves with this rigorous demand [that there should be no rapprochement on the part of the actor between his acting and his normal personality] is a loss of distance through over-distancing. What we get, then, is a theater from which all tension and antinomy has been removed, and which is demonstrating situations of a mere factual nature and relationship" (p. 286). "Brecht wants to over-distance in order to prevent any *Einfühling,* any empathy on the part of actors and audience" (p. 286). See Brecht's own novel, *Dreigrossenroman* (1934).

16. Ilie, *La novelística,* 201.

Notes to Chapter 6

1. Barcelona, Noguer, 1955. This is the only edition to date. *La catira* is billed as the first title in the series, "Historias de Venezuela." However, like *La colmena,* it remains without a sequel.

2. Kirsner, in *The Novels and Travels,* observes, "*La Catira* exotically, and perhaps superficially so, dedicates itself to the portrayal of primitive

life in the wilds of Venezuela. In its attempt to intone epic qualities, the novel at its best succeeds in becoming a fantasy, at its worst, a sort of unwilling *esperpento*" (p. 93). How a novel can become "willingly" or "unwillingly" is not explained. Arturo Torres-Rioseco, in "Camilo José Cela, primer novelista español contemporáneo," *Revista hispánica moderna*, 28 (April-October, 1962), 166–71, has carried the innocuous comparison with the *esperpento* a step further to make what could constitute an important statement on Cela's intent:

"Es muy probable que Cela, invitado por el gobierno venezolano de la dictadura a escribir una novela nacional, partiera originalmente con la idea de escribir un esperpento a la manera de Valle-Inclán. Pero no se pueden dictar términos ni limitaciones a un escritor tan intenso como Cela. El esperpento se convertió en una novela humana, fuerte, terrígena. [. . .] El enfoque de *La Catira* es, por supuesto, satírico; ya dijimos que el plan primario debe de haber sido de esperpento. Otra vez insistimos en que el gran afecto que siente el autor por la gente de los llanos le destruyó el intento inicial. Cabría preguntarse: ¿Trató Cela de hacer en la persona de la Catira la anti-Bárbara? Valdría la pena detenerse ante este problema. Una cosa sí podemos asegurar: *La Catira* no es un *pastiche*, sino una interpretación real de aspectos de la vida nacional, muy superior, tanto en la fórmula lingüística como en el tonelaje psicológico a la de muchos novelistas venezolanos" (pp. 169–70). Torres offers no significant evidence in support of his contention regarding the original intent of Cela in *La catira*, and this study will overlook his observation as untenable.

3. Martín Marco cannot be called a focal point because he is in no way more outstanding or more important than any other character in the novel. He just appears more frequently. And, unlike Pipía Sánchez, he does not transcend his situation, he is not uniquely symbolic, and he is neither consciously aware of nor articulate about his position.

4. The Latin-American novel of the collective unconscious has often taken the extremely imaginative form of *realismo mágico*; nevertheless, the concept as the intellectual basis of a movement in the novel has yet to be adequately discussed. Ángel Flores, in "Magical Realism in Spanish American Fiction," *Hispania*, 38 (May, 1955), 187–92, was one of the first to use this term in criticism, although the common understanding of it has gone beyond his original definition. José Antonio Portuondo, *El heroísmo intelectual*, 133–39, gives a summary of some of the early authors within this current as well as some of the directions it has taken.

5. The most respected of the Marxist critics has been Georg Lukács, whose highly valued critical writings continually reiterate the social ethic of literature. See Víctor Flores Olea, "Lukács y el problema del arte," *Revista de la Universidad de México*, 17 (August, 1963), 6–10. Unfortunately, Flores does not go beyond a presentation of Lukács' theories to discuss them as they are being practiced in the novel today, overlooking entirely a blooming garden at his own doorstep, so to speak. Several other Latin-American writers, however, have spoken out in one voice with Lukács. See Portuondo and, among others, Augusto Roa Bastos, "El fuego en las manos," *Diálogo*, 2ª época, No. 1 (April, 1960), 17–18. Although I have not had the opportunity to read it, I understand that J. M. Castellet, in *La hora del lector*, echoes many of Lukács' theories. Castellet is one of the most sympathetic commentators on Cela's work.

6. From Lukács, as quoted by Flores Olea, "Lukács y el problema del arte," 8.

7. See José Antonio Pérez Regalado, Doña Bárbara *y* La catira. *Dos novelas sobre el llano venezolano.*

8. Alborg, *Hora actual,* 79–113. "Camilo José Cela," denies that Cela has succeeded in giving Venezuela a new archetype. His comments take advantage of the protest launched against the language and the theme, adding his own interpretation of the artistic circumstances, which he calls futile. Juan Echevarría Uribe, in "Historias de Venezuela. *La catira,* por Camilo José Cela," *Anales de la Universidad de Chile,* 114 (1956), 144–46, agrees with Alborg: "Cela ha hecho un enorme esfuerzo de mimetismo filológico, sociológico y literario para realizar esta última obra. El gran escritor de *La familia de Pascual Duarte* se defiende bien en cada página pero no logra, lástima grande, crearnos un ambiente literario auténtico ni una heroína simbólica e imperecedera como la Bárbara del novelista venezolano" (p. 145).

9. Prjevalinsky, *El sistema estético*: "La forma es de gran belleza, hay mágnificas metáforas y expresiones parcialmente metafóricas que embelescan. La naturaleza, el folklore, la observación psicológica, el latir de la vida, se transforman en poesía y emoción. Hallamos, con frequencia, que estos párrafos vibrantes de sentir se desarrollan con arreglo a moldes de geometrización estética, en masas de distribución equilibrada, que Cela ha empleado con variedad y profusión a través de esta obra" (p. 171). Mrs. Prjevalinsky's work is an extended study of the stylistic characteristics of *La catira,* which she rightly believes to be found to lesser or greater degree in all of Cela's works. Topics considered are: "La antítesis," "La reiteración," "La adjetivación y las pluralidades cualitativas. Estructura y función," "Las series de calificativos y los conjuntos semejantes," "La expresión metafórica," "La metáfora." The foregoing list of chapters comes under the heading of "La estructura en función de la expresividad." This main concern is followed by several chapters grouped around the heading "Una exégesis de temas y fenómenos literarios." Here the critic attempts to defend her recognition of certain themes, on the basis of the stylistic elements established for the novel as a whole. This study is particularly useful in these latter sections, which give a broad perspective to the discussions and represent a solid contribution to the study of Cela's works.

10. Ilie, in *La novelística,* "El ritmo narrativo," 209–13, concludes: "El experimento celiano de estructura oral hace al lector suponer las circunstancias en que el relato es recitado, más que leído" (p. 212).

11. Ilie has discussed the pessimistic overtones of the novel, "La primacia del instinto," 217–28, taking up again the theme of anticivilization first discussed at length in his chapter on *Nuevas andanzas y desventuras de Lazarillo de Tormes.*

12. Carlos Otero, "La catira, novela de Camilo José Cela," *Cuadernos hispanoamericanos,* 25 (1956), 352.

13. It is important not to confuse Cela's predictable approach to a given situation with extraordinary circumstances indicative of either a satire or an *esperpento.* The reader who is familiar with Cela through *La colmena* and *Nuevas andanzas y desventuras de Lazarillo de Tormes* will find nothing singular in the following passage, one of the first in the novel and a sketch of Pipía Sánchez' first husband-to-be:

"Don Filiberto era poeta y ensayista. Don Filiberto también era versado en historia. Don Filiberto cuidaba, hasta donde le era posible hacerlo, de que el joropo no se adulterase.

[. . .]Don Filiberto Marqués era autor de un libro – *Valsiao, escobillao y zapatiado*, Ediciones Camorue, Barquisimeto, 1935 — en el que trataba de la pureza del joropo. El libro tiene ciento cinco páginas y va dedicado al arpisto Manuel Colmenares y el cantor Gregorio Páez, de San Francisco de Asís, Estado Aragua.

Don Filiberto, algunas veces, cepillaba su borsalino de peloeguama y se acercaba a Caracas. Don Filiberto, por más que anduviera por la capital, no perdía su buen aire campeche" (pp. 17–18). The two dominant characteristics of this and other passages that Torres may have had in mind are the language and the tone (see note 3). The repetitive and symmetrical patterns occur throughout the novel as a stylistic constant. Being uniformly distributed, they are not unique to the first part of the novel. At the same time Cela's tone, indicative of his position with respect to his subject matter, is the familiar aloof one, the product of his belief that the novelist should observe but not sympathize nor identify with his characters and their circumstances. What is common to a larger collection of examples is not distinctive for any one. If the foregoing quotation is indicative of the tone of *La catira*, Cela's position with respect to his subject and personalities in this novel is no different from that in his other works.

14. With regard to "primitive languages" and formal patterning, see C. F. Voegelin, "Casual and Noncasual Utterances with Unified Structure," in Thomas A. Sebeok, *Style in Language*, 57–68.

15. Ilie, *La novelística*, 209.

16. See Ilie, *La novelística*, 217–28, also 215–17 on the supernatural.

17. Cela as an outsider may be present in his novel in the person of the Galician Evaristo: "En una de sus visitas a Caracas, a don Filiberto le presentaron a un gallego medio vagabundo, que se llamaba Evaristo. Evaristo, antes, cuando era persona de provecho se llamaba Camilo" (p. 18). Later, Evaristo affirms, "Sí, señor, yo le vengo a ser de Iria" (120). Cela was born in Iria Flavia, Galicia. I mention this, not because it is important but because of the interesting sidelight it throws on Cela and what he is capable of doing. Kirsner, however, in *The Novels and Travels*, considers this aspect of the novel extremely important and discusses at length what he believes to be Cela's role *in* novel: "More than any other of his novels, *La Catira* presents a portrait of Cela forging a novel. In this work the author is one of his own characters" (p. 94). "Ever present in *La Catira*, be it in its literary content or in its appendix, is the personality of Cela, the Spaniard relating himself to his own intimate environment of language and life" (p. 95). "Viewed as an account of the author's travels in a strange land, *La Catira* acquires another dimension. The work then becomes the literary experience of a voyageur in search of spiritual refuge. In this case, of one who must endeavor to escape the agony of Spain" (p. 99). I suspect that here, as elsewhere in Kirsner's study, my failure to discover the basis for his statements lies in what must be our totally different views on the nature of literature.

18. See Moseley, *Pseudonyms of Christ in the Modern Novel*. Many of Mr. Moseley's examples, in my opinion, are forced and demonstrate the dangers of the myth criticism. Nevertheless, his book is interesting and valuable for the avenues of investigation it explores and the further research it suggests.

19. For this reason I cannot agree with Carlos Otero, who writes: "El deslumbramiento de Cela ante la Naturaleza americana — y ante la palabra, como luego se verá — es total. Cela 'se amaniguó' sin remedio, como no podía menos de suceder, y buena prueba de ello son las numerosas descripciones, vivas de color, del paisaje llanero. Y empatió desde el principio, y

hacia lo hondo, con aquellas gentes, a las que, a pesar de su pretendida objetividad de buen novelista, se ve que admira profundamente, y, a la postre, le inspiran una gran ternura" (p. 353). Certainly this is true in that it offers an explanation as to why Cela bothered with the novel at all; but in ignoring the techniques of the novel for distancing and reader-alienation, Otero gives a false impression of the work.

Notes to Chapter 7

1. Our text is that of the first edition (Barcelona, Noguer, 1962).
2. Writing in the literary review Cela directs, Antonio Fernández Molina, in "En su tobogán," *Papeles de Son Armadans*, 19 (May, 1963), 191–206, affirms that it is "una intensa novela, una curiosa novela, una de las novelas más audaces que se hayan dado en castellano y aún en la literatura universal" (p. 191). Furthermore, "Un alarde técnico semejante no es fácil encontrarlo en otra novela en castellano si se exceptúa, claro está, *Mrs. Caldwell habla con su hijo*, que toda ella es una audacia pura y que está llena de aciertos convulsionantes" (p. 198).
3. In the *Prólogo*, Cela states: "Estas páginas tuvieron muchos títulos provisionales hasta que me decidí por el que dejo, y que es el que me parece más apropiado al resbaladizo sentimiento de hambre (no física sino moral) de la turbamulta de personajes que actúan en su antiheroico y doméstico escenario" (p. 18).
4. Another very interesting difference between *La colmena* and *Tobogán de hambrientos* deserves brief mention: the author's respect, as a human being, for the people whom he portrays. In *La colmena* Cela maintains a strict detachment. The author does not pronounce value judgments upon the behavior of his characters or upon their emotions in the face of life, although there is a necessary implied judgment in the very nature and content of the work. In *Tobogán de hambrientos* Cela sometimes appears to look not unkindly upon his characters:

"Nabetse Ledif bajó la cabeza muy resignadamente, cogió los diez duros que le daban y, cuando el local acabó de desalojarse, salió un pie tras otro y sin decir palabra, por el camino de Tomelloso. Nabetse Ledif, por la carretera abajo y envuelto en las sombras de la noche, semejaba un fantasma acorralado y sin rumbo: como los astros que ruedan, muertos y desde hace miles de años, por los más remotos y heladores confines del universo" (p. 35). If it is true that Cela's attitude toward his characters as expressed in lyrical interludes such as the preceding is different in this novel, it nevertheless does not constitute identification or sympathizing with them. For the most part, Cela's irony and the "law of the jungle" remain in effect. Cela (as Cela) says: "Esta vida es un fandango y el que pregunta se queda de cuadra. Corolario: el que no llora mama, y cada uno estornuda como Dios le ayuda" (p. 83).

5. See, for example, 254, 294, 295, 304, 308, 311, 327, 337, among others.
6. Fernández Molina in "En su tobogán," elaborates on this further in conjunction with arguments to show the "moral and therapeutic" intent of Cela's novel: "El mundo que nos retrata Cela no es ni puede ser sino el que conoce y padece a diario, el que también le afirma como hombre, como escritor y que a un tiempo le sirve de tormento y de espectáculo (el que culpa tiene) entretenido. El escritor es ya un filósofo, un humorista y a estas alturas no se asusta de nada. Toma nota de la realidad, que es la verdad y nos ofrece una serie de tipos en los que podemos reconocernos y corregirnos"

(p. 195). "Cela, deliberadamente, como un fotógrafo de pueblo, hace la fotografía de los elementos de una sociedad que presenta como ejemplo a corregir, no se burla de ella y si señala sus defectos es porque los siente como algo muy suyo, lo que se burla pero que sin duda no vería con buenos ojos que las burlas partieran de alguien que no participara del parentesco" (p. 199).

7. At the same time, Cela makes occasional references to the fact that he is the author and as such is composing the novel. He is challenged at one point:

> —Esa sabia sentencia, ¿de quién la copió usted?
>
> —De nadie, ¡a ver qué se ha creído! ¿Usted no me supone capaz de inventar sentencias?
>
> —Pues hombre, la verdad: no mucho. Así como mayores síntomas, no le había notado. ¡Qué quiere que le diga! (p. 47)

Several similar exchanges occur, affirming Cela's position as the writer.

8. Compare Sarraute's statement in *L'ère du soupcon*:

"Tout est là, en effet: reprendre au lecteur son bien et l'attirer coûte que coûte sur le terrain de l'auteur. Pour y parvenir, le procédé qui consiste à désigner par un 'je' le héros principal, constitue un moyen à la fois efficace et facile, et, pour cette raison, sans doute, si fréquemment employe.

Alors le lecteur est d'un coup à l'intérieur, à la place même où l'auteur se trouve, à une profondeur où rien ne subsiste de ces points de repère commodes à l'aide desquels il construit les personnages. Il est plongé et maintenu jusqu'au bout dans une matière anonyme comme le sang, dans un magma sans nom, sans contours. S'il parvient à se diriger, c'est grâce aux jalons que l'auteur a posés pour s'y reconnaître. Nulle réminiscence de son monde familier, nul souci conventionnel de cohésion ou de vraisemblance, ne détourne son attention ni ne freine son effort. Les seules limites auxquelles, comme l'auteur, il se heurte, sont celles qui sont inhérentes à toute recherche de cet ordre ou qui sont propres à la vision de l'auteur" (pp. 73–74).

In terms of Cela's artificial levels in *Tobogán de hambrientos*, these remarks are more closely applicable to the internal "audience" than they are to the external reader. From a practical point of view, however, these two levels are the same, and Miss Sarraute's observations of a general tendency in the contemporary novel seem to bespeak Cela's intent in this novel.

9. Compare the following: "El Sebas, el de telégrafos, fue un hombre del montón; un hombre como todos: corriente, moliente y contribuyente; un hombre que, de no haber nacido, nadie lo hubiera echado a faltar. Claro es que esto también puede decirse de Cristóbal Colón, y de Cervantes, y de Isaac Peral, y de todos; cuando un hombre no nace, nadie lo echa de menos, porque nadie, tampoco, puede saber hasta dónde habría de llegar su chispa" (p. 427).

10. Cela's hilariously funny account of the content and fame of the novel makes one wonder how anyone could call Cela's works "tremendistas" and put them in the same class with this woman's "art."

11. In my opinion this is the principal drawback of Kirsner's *The Novels and Travels*.

12. There is more than just a passing affinity between Cela and his controversial compatriot Luis Buñuel, the movie maker whose *Los olvidados* and *Viridiana* have been internationally acclaimed despite their frightening insistence upon man's inherent and immutable primitive instinct.

13. Fernández Molina, in "En su tobogán," notes very perceptively in this respect that: "hace mucho tiempo que pasó la época del héroe y ahora se ha ido más allá de recurrir al antihéroe y se anda por los dominios del infrahéroe. Y

esto en el fondo no es sino un cambio de enfoque, pues de los mismos tipos humanos que antaño se les cargó de transcendencia, hoy se les retrata desde el punto de vista que les corresponde como un número más. Cela se esfuerza por salvar lo que de personal e intransferible hay en cada anécdota, pero no puede por menos que dar testimonios de la realidad y, al mismo tiempo que de la diferencia, de la semejanza, al menos de tono y altura, que hay en la mayor parte de las peripecias humanas" (p. 205).

14. *Mrs. Caldwell habla con su hijo*, 2ª ed. (Barcelona, 1958).

15. *Papeles de Son Armadans*, Mallorca.

16. *La colmena*, 4ª ed. (Barcelona, Noguer, 1962), 11–12.

17. A full-dress study of the function of humor and the comic in Cela's novels and in post-Civil War Spanish literature is badly needed. In passing, one might mention the use of comedy by Cela for possible corrective measures and a similar function of comedy advanced by Henri Bergson, "Laughter," in Wylie Sypher, ed., *Comedy* (Garden City, N.Y., 1956), 61–190. Fernández Molina, in his article, "En su tobogán," speaks of a relation between Cela and the "humor negro" of André Breton. A common basis in twentieth-century life and letters also fosters a recognizable resemblance between Cela and the American "black humorists." See "The Black Humorists," *Time*, 85 (February 12, 1965), 94–96. American authors discussed include James Purdy, Joseph Heller, Bruce Jay Friedman, John Barth, and J. P. Donleavy.

18. Fernández Molina, "En su tobogán," 195, 199.

19. *Garito de hospicianos* (Barcelona, Noguer, 1963).

20. Francisco Umbral, "Camilo José Cela: *Garito de hospicianos*," *Impreso en España*, No. 12 (February 29, 1964), 96.

21. Fernández Molina, "En su tobogán," 202.

22. Madrid, Alfaguara, 1965.

23. Concerning the structural pattern of *Tobogán de hambrientos* and *La familia del héroe*, see my article, "Intrinsic and Extrinsic Pattern in Two 'New Novels' of Camilo José Cela," *Papers on Language and Literature*, to be published.

Notes to Conclusion

1. In the Introduction to *Mrs. Caldwell habla con su hijo*, 2ª ed., Cela discusses his novels in terms of experiments with varying modes of fictional expression.

2. Oscar Büdel, "Contemporary Theater and Aesthetic Distance," *PMLA*, 76 (June, 1961), 277–91.

Selected Bibliography

Texts

Cela, Camilo José, *Caminos inciertos. La colmena*, 4ª ed. Barcelona, Noguer, 1962.

———, *La familia de Pascual Duarte*, 14ª ed. Barcelona, Destino, 1963.

———, *La familia de Pascual Duarte*, Harold L. Boudreau and John W. Kronik, eds. New York, Appleton-Century-Crofts, Inc., 1961.

———, *La familia del héroe*. Madrid, Alfaguara, 1965.

———, *Garito de hospicianos*. Barcelona, Noguer, 1963.

———, *Historias de Venezuela. La catira*. Barcelona, Noguer, 1955.

———, *Mrs. Caldwell habla con su hijo*, 2ª ed. Barcelona, Destino, 1958.

———, *Nuevas andanzas y desventuras de Lazarillo de Tormes*, 6ª ed. Barcelona, Noguer, 1955.

———, *Pabellón de reposo*, 3ª ed. Barcelona, Destino, 1957.

———, *Tobogán de hambrientos*. Barcelona, Noguer, 1962.

Criticism in General

Alborg, Juan Luis, *Hora actual de la novela española*, [1ª serie]. Madrid, Taurus, 1959.

Allen, Walter, *The Modern Novel in Britain and the United States*. New York, E. P. Dutton & Co., Inc., 1965.

Baquero Goyanes, Mariano, *Proceso de la novela actual*. Madrid, Rialp, 1963.

Booth, Wayne C., *The Rhetoric of Fiction*. Chicago, University of Chicago Press, 1961.

Büdel, Oscar, "Contemporary Theater and Aesthetic Distance." *PMLA*, 75 (June, 1961), 277–91.

Castellet, José María, *La hora del lector*. Barcelona, Seix y Barral, 1957.

———, "La joven novela española." *Sur*, No. 284 (September–October, 1963), 48–54.

Cela, Camilo José, *Cuatro figuras del 98*. Barcelona, Aedos, 1961.

———, "Dos tendencias de la nueva literatura española." *Papeles de Son Armadans*, 27 (October, 1962), 3–20.

Chase, Richard, *Quest for Myth*. Baton Rouge, Louisiana State University Press, 1949.

Church, Margaret, *Time and Reality*. Chapel Hill, University of North Carolina Press, 1963.

Edel, Leon, *The Modern Psychological Novel*. New York, Grove Press, 1959.

Eoff, Sherman, H., *The Modern Spanish Novel, Comparative Essays Examining the Impact of Science on Fiction*. New York, New York University Press, 1961.

Flores, Ángel, "Magical Realism in Spanish American Fiction." *Hispania*, 38 (May, 1955), 187–92.

Flores Olea, Víctor, "Lukács y el problema del arte." *Revista de la Universidad de México*, 17 (August, 1963), 6–10.

Frye, Northrup, *Anatomy of Criticism*. Princeton, Princeton University Press, 1957.

Glicksberg, Charles I., *The Self in Modern Literature*. University Park, Pennsylvania State University Press, 1963.

———, *The Tragic Vision in Twentieth-Century Literature*. Carbondale, Southern Illinois University Press, 1963.

Gómez Lance, Betty Rita, "La actitud picaresca en la novela española del siglo XX." Unpublished Ph.D. dissertation, Washington University, 1960.

Goodman, Paul, *The Structure of Literature*. Chicago, University of Chicago Press, 1954.

Grupp, William J., "Contemporary Spanish Literary and Intellectual Life." *Modern Language Journal*, 45 (April, 1961), 156–60.

Harvey, W. J., *Character and the Novel*. Ithaca, Cornell University Press, 1965.

Humphrey, Robert, *Stream of Consciousness in the Modern Novel*. Berkeley, University of California Press, 1954.

Jones, Willis Knapp, "Recent Novels of Spain: 1936–56." *Hispania*, 40 (September, 1957), 303–11.

Laín Entralgo, Pedro, *La generación de noventa y ocho*. Madrid, Espasa-Calpe, 1959.

Leary, Lewis, *Contemporary Literary Scholarship: A Critical Review*. New York, Appleton-Century-Crofts, Inc., 1958.

Le Sage, Laurent, *The French New Novel: An Introduction and a Sampler*. University Park, Pennsylvania State University Press, 1962.

Lewis, Richard W. B., *The Picaresque Saint*. Philadelphia, J. B. Lippincott Company, 1959.

Livingstone, Leon, "Interior Duplication and the Problem of Form in the Modern Spanish Novel." *PMLA*, 73 (September, 1958), 393–406.

McElroy, Davis Dunbar, *Existentialism and Modern Literature*. New York, Philosophical Library, 1963.

McMahon, Dorothy, "Humor in Nadal-Award Spanish Novels." *Kentucky Foreign Language Quarterly*, 7 (1961), 75–84.

Mallo, Jerónimo, "Caracterización y valor del 'tremendismo' en la novela española contemporánea." *Hispania*, 34 (March, 1956), 49–55.

Mendilow, A. A., *Time and the Novel*. London, P. Nevill, 1952.

Meyerhoff, Hans, *Time in Literature*. Berkeley, University of California Press, 1955.

Miller, James E., Jr., *Myth and Method: Modern Theories of Fiction*. Lincoln, University of Nebraska Press, 1960.

Moseley, Edwin M., *Pseudonyms of Christ in the Modern Novel*. Pittsburgh, The University of Pittsburg Press, 1962.

Nora, Eugenio G. de, *La novela española contemporánea (1927–1960)*. Madrid, Gredos, 1962.

O'Connor, William Van, *Forms of Modern Fiction.* Minneapolis, University of Minnesota Press, 1948.
Pacifici, Sergio, *A Guide to Contemporary Italian Literature.* Cleveland, Meridian Books, 1962.
Palley, Julian, "Existentialist Trends in the Modern Spanish Novel." *Hispania,* 44 (March, 1961), 21–26.
Pérez Minik, Domingo, *Novelistas españoles de los siglos XIX, XX.* Madrid, Guadarrama, 1957.
Portuondo, José Antonio, *El heroísmo intelectual.* México, Tezontle, 1955.
Praag-Chantraine, Jacqueline van, "Chronique des lettres espagnoles: actualité du roman picaresque." *Synthèses,* 14 (May, 1959), 121–33.
[Prjevalinsky, Olga] Ferrer, Olga P., "La literatura española tremendista y su nexo con el existencialismo." *Revista hispánica moderna,* 22 (July-October, 1956), 297–303.
Ransom, John Crowe, *The New Criticism.* Norfolk, Conn., New Directions, 1941.
Roa Bastos, Augusto, "El fuego en las manos." *Diálogo,* 2ª época, No. 1 (April, 1960), 17–18.
Robbe-Grillet, Alain, *Pour un nouveau roman.* Paris, Editions de minuit, 1963.
Romberg, Bertil, *Studies in the Narrative Technique of the First-Person Novel.* Stockholm, Alqvist and Wiksell, 1962.
Sánchez, José, "Los premios literarios españoles." *Kentucky Foreign Language Quarterly,* 6 (1959), 189–94.
Sarraute, Nathalie, *L'ère du soupçon.* Paris, Gallimard, 1956.
Sebeok, Thomas A., *Style in Language, the Proceedings of an Interdisciplinary Conference on Verbal Style and the Literary Process.* Cambridge, The Technology Press of the Massachusetts Institute of Technology, 1960.
Torrente Ballester, Gonzalo, *Panorama de la literatura española contemporánea.* Madrid, Guadarrama, 1956.
Urbanski, Edmund Stephen, "El revisionismo en la valoración de las letras y cultura contemporánea de España." *Hispania,* 48 (December, 1965), 816–25.
Vilá Selam, José, *Tres ensayos sobre la literatura y nuestra guerra.* Madrid, Nacional, 1956.
Wade, Gerald E., "The Cult of Violence in the Contemporary Spanish Novel." *University of Tennessee Studies in the Humanities,* I (1956), 51–58.
Wellek, René, *Concepts of Criticism.* New Haven, Yale University Press, 1963.

Criticism on Cela

Beck, Mary Ann, "Nuevo encuentro con «La familia de Pascual Duarte»." *Revista hispánica moderna,* 30 (July-October, 1964), 279–98.
Castellet, J. M., "Iniciación a la obra narrativa de Camilo José Cela." *Revista hispánica moderna,* 28 (April-October, 1962), 107–50.
Cela, Camilo José, "La experiencia personal en *Pabellón de reposo.*" *Papeles de Son Armadans,* 24 (February, 1962), 131–35.
———, "Notas sobra la herramienta literaria." *Papeles de Son Armadans,* 24 (March, 1962), 243–46.
———, "Pascual Duarte, de limpio." *Papeles de Son Armadans,* 21 (June, 1961), 227–31.
———, "Relativo curriculum vitae." *Revista hispánica moderna,* 28 (April-October, 1962), 179–275.

Corriols, Joseph F., "An Analysis of the 'Tremendismo' in the Novels of Camilo José Cela." Unpublished Master's thesis, Duquesne University, 1959.

Durán, Manuel, "La estructura de *La colmena.*" *Hispania,* 43 (March, 1960), 19–24.

Eoff, Sherman, "Tragedy of the Unwanted Person, in Three Versions: Pablo de Segovia, Pito Pérez, Pascual Duarte." *Hispania,* 39 (May, 1956), 190–96.

Feldman, David M., "Camilo José Cela and 'La familia de Pascual Duarte'." *Hispania,* 44 (December, 1961), 656–59.

Fernández Molina, Antonio, "En su tobogán." *Papeles de Son Armadans,* 29 (May, 1963), 191–206.

Flasher, John J., "Aspects of Novelistic Technique in Cela's *La colmena.*" *West Virginia University Philological Papers,* 21 (November, 1959), 30–43.

Foster, David William, "Cela's Changing Concept of the Novel." *Hispania,* 49 (May, 1966), 244–49.

———, "*La colmena* de Camilo José Cela y los informes de éste sobre la novela." *Hispanófila,* to be published.

———, "Camilo José Cela. *La familia del héroe.*" *Books Abroad,* 40 (Summer, 1966), 318–19.

———, "Intrinsic and Extrinsic Pattern in Two 'New Novels' by Camilo José Cela." *Papers on Language and Literature,* to be published.

Gómez de la Serna, Gaspar, "Camilo José Cela: *Mrs. Caldwell habla con su hijo.*" *Clavileño,* 5 (January-February, 1954), 76–77.

Gómez Santos, Marino, *Camilo José Cela.* Barcelona, Cliper, 1958.

Ilie, Paul, *La novelística de Camilo José Cela.* Madrid, Gredos, 1963.

———, "Primitivismo y vagabundaje en la obra de C. J. Cela." *Ínsula,* No. 170 (January, 1961), 14.

Kirsner, Robert, *The Novels and Travels of Camilo José Cela.* Chapel Hill, University of North Carolina Press, 1963.

———, "Spain in the Novels of Cela and Baroja." *Hispania,* 41 (March, 1958), 39–41.

Marañón, Gregorio, "Prólogo a 'La familia de Pascual Duarte'." *Ínsula,* No. 5 (1946), 1, 3.

Martínez, Bueno, Gustavo, "*La colmena,* novela behaviorista." *Clavileño,* III (September-October, 1952), 53–58.

Ortega, José, "La expresión de la nada en *La colmena* de C. J. Cela." Unpublished Ph.D. dissertation, Ohio State University, 1964.

———, "Importancia del personaje Martín Marco en *La colmena* de Cela." *Romance Notes,* 7 (Spring, 1965), 92–95.

Otero, Carlos, "La catira, novela de Camilo José Cela." *Cuadernos hispanoamericanos,* 25 (1956), 351–56.

Pérez Regalado, José Antonio, Doña Bárbara *y* La catira, *dos novelas sobre el llano venezolano.* Santa Cruz de Tenerife, Orinoco, 1960.

Predmore, R. L., "La imagen del hombre en las obras de Camilo José Cela." *La torre,* 9 (January-March, 1961), 81–102.

Prjevalinsky, Olga, *El sistema estético de Camilo José Cela, expresividad y estructura.* Valencia, Castalia, 1960.

Rand, Marguerite C., "Lazarillo de Tormes, Classic and Contemporary." *Hispania,* 44 (May, 1961), 222–29.

Shaw, D. L., "[Review of Alonso Zamora Vicente's *Camilo José Cela*]." *Bulletin of Hispanic Studies,* 40 (1963), 257–58.

Torre, Guillermo de, "Vagabundeos críticos por el mundo de Cela." *Revista hispánica moderna*, 28 (April-October, 1962), 151–65.

Torres-Rioseco, Arturo, "Camilo José Cela, primer novelista español contemporáneo." *Revista hispánica moderna*, 28 (April-October, 1962), 166–71.

Trives, Eduardo, *Una semana con Camilo José Cela*. Alicante, Vidal, 1960.

Umbral, Francisco, "Camilo José Cela: *Garito de Hospicianos*." *Impreso en España*, No. 12 (February 29, 1964), 96.

Uribe Echevarría, Juan, "Historias de Venezuela. *La catira*, por Camilo José Cela." *Anales de la Universidad de Chile*, 114 (1956), 144–45.

Veliz V., Irma, "Camilo José Cela, novelista español contemporáneo." Unpublished thesis, Universidad de Chile, 1954.

Zamora Vicente, Alonso, *Camilo José Cela (acercamiento a un escritor)*. Madrid, Gredos, 1962.

Index

This index excludes titles of works cited in the text, notes, and bibliography other than the novels of Cela.